MW01285896

Western Illinois University
School of Law Enforcement and Justice Administration
LEJA 520 Course Syllabus

Course Information

Course Title: Restorative Justice
Course Number: LEJA 520

Faculty Information

Name: Barry S. McCrary, Ed.D.
Phone Number: 309-298-1220
E-mail: bs-mccrary@wiu.edu

Course Description:

This course reviews the evolution and development of what has come to be known as Restorative Justice. The learning experience will address a variety of topics including restorative justice principles, community engagement, victim issues, and restorative practices and change. This workbook is a collection of various articles for class discussion and research.

Upon completion of this course, our graduates will be able to:

1. Demonstrate an understanding of restorative justice concepts, principles, and values.
2. Recognize the traumatic impact of crime on victims, communities, and offenders, and ways to be responsive to the needs and interest of crime victims.
3. Explain the configuration, methods, and potential uses of various restorative practices and evaluate the degree to which they are more or less restorative.
4. Identify several practical strategies for developing active partnerships within the community.
5. Manage personal, interpersonal, and organizational change and prepare strategies for addressing the response to change efforts.
6. Develop the first steps of a plan of action.

Module One: *Restorative Justice concepts, principles, and values*

	Details
Objectives	**1.1** Identify the elements present in an effective conflict resolution process.
	1.2 Describe the principles and values of restorative justice.
	1.3 Name the three primary stakeholders in the restorative justice process.
	1.4 Describe the role of accountability in restorative justice process.

Western Illinois University
School of Law Enforcement and Justice Administration
LEJA 520 Course Syllabus

Course Information
Course Title: Restorative Justice
Course Number: LEJA 520

Faculty Information
Name: Barry S. McCrary, Ed.D.
Phone Number: 309-298-1220
E-mail: bs-mccrary@wiu.edu

Course Description:

This course reviews the evolution and development of what has come to be known as Restorative Justice. The learning experience will address a variety of topics including restorative justice principles, community engagement, victim issues, and restorative practices and change. This workbook is a collection of various articles for class discussion and research.

Upon completion of this course, our graduates will be able to:

1. Demonstrate an understanding of restorative justice concepts, principles, and values.
2. Recognize the traumatic impact of crime on victims, communities, and offenders, and ways to be responsive to the needs and interest of crime victims.
3. Explain the configuration, methods, and potential uses of various restorative practices and evaluate the degree to which they are more or less restorative.
4. Identify several practical strategies for developing active partnerships within the community.
5. Manage personal, interpersonal, and organizational change and prepare strategies for addressing the response to change efforts.
6. Develop the first steps of a plan of action.

Module *Two: Impact of crime on victims, communities, and offenders*	
	Details
Objectives	**1.1** Recognize the impact of crime on victims. **1.2** Recognize the characteristics, needs and interest of victims from the positions of empowerment and disempowerment. **1.3** Understand how the criminal justice system, and other systems may serve victims of crime differently, depending upon the status of the victim in society. **1.4** Explain how participants in the criminal justice system can negatively impact victims. **1.5** Identify what victims expect from the criminal justice system. **1.6** Describe appropriate ways to communicate, work, and connect with victims.

What are the effects for victim, offender and community?

Restorative justice emerged as part of a search for a better way to respond to crime. In this article, we'll explore the research to find out whether RJ can achieve this ambitious aim. How do victims respond to restorative justice? What is the impact on offenders and on reoffending? And how can the community benefit from restorative practices?

How do victims respond to restorative justice?

Research indicates that the restorative approach has the potential to successfully respond to various victim needs.

For instance, participation in complementary restorative interventions has been found to be therapeutic for victims, particularly for victims of violent crime. Compared to victims whose case was only dealt with in the conventional judicial system, victims who also got to experience RJ reported significantly lower levels of anger and fear. Victim-participants have further credited restorative interventions for allowing them to move on from victimisation and for promoting empowerment.

Victims are also more likely to receive compensation for material damages, symbolic reparation and an apology than in a conventional court. This is important as it provides recognition and acknowledgment of the harm victims experienced.

It is, therefore, not entirely surprising that studies generally report high levels of victim satisfaction with RJ. Restorative interventions are often found to be more satisfying than traditional criminal justice proceedings and victim-participants would recommend them to other victims.

In a study conducted with victims of violent crime, educator Tinneke Van Camp found that they particularly appreciated the chance they had to express their emotions and concerns, tell their story and ask the offender questions. They found this liberating. Moreover, the fact that participation is voluntary is in itself empowering and a reason for satisfaction. Victims in my study explained that they often felt excluded from the criminal justice system but in the restorative intervention they felt in control because of the opportunity to make choices about their involvement. They also valued the interaction with, and support from, the restorative facilitator in the preparatory phase and during the face-to-face meeting.

Although a minority of victims who agreed to participate in RJ have reported a negative emotional impact following participation, comparative and evaluative research findings suggest that RJ outperforms traditional criminal justice proceedings in meeting victims' needs.

What is the impact on offenders and on reoffending?

Different studies have demonstrated that offenders generally tend to comply (fully or partially) with the outcome agreement that resulted from VOM or conferencing and that offender satisfaction is high.

In a study conducted by Week 3 educator Joanna Shapland and colleagues (including Week 6 educators Gwen Robinson and Angela Sorsby in 2011, offender-participants reported that they were satisfied with the outcome. They also agreed that RJ was a good way to deal with offending and would recommend it to others. They said that the confrontation and dialogue with their victim allowed a better understanding of the consequences of victimisation and encouraged them to address the problems related to their offending. There is, however, the potential of feeling overwhelmed and overpowered at the conference itself, especially among young offenders. Daly (2003) highlights that young offenders might not find it easy to engage and navigate the RJ approach and feel powerless when confronted with their victim, the victim's supporters, and community volunteers.

Of course, policy-makers, who allocate funding to criminal justice reform, are most interested in the effectiveness of RJ in preventing reoffending, particularly in an age of austerity. It is always difficult to measure reoffending, and within the limits of such measures, findings remain tentative but encouraging.

Joanna Shapland and her colleagues (2011) studied restorative conferencing programmes that involved adult offenders who had committed relatively serious offences in England and Wales and found a significant decrease in the frequency of reconviction following participation in conferencing. They also report no significant results pointing towards any criminogenic effects, meaning that RJ does not make offenders worse.

Sherman and Strang (2007) clarify that RJ substantially reduces reoffending for some types of offences, but not for all. They conclude that RJ works best for more serious crime (particularly those involving interpersonal violence) and is unlikely to cause more reoffending than conventional criminal justice proceedings.

At this point, it is important to note that desistance from crime (the process through which people cease and refrain from offending) is a process, not a moment. Shapland and her colleagues point to the possibility of RJ *consolidating* an ongoing move towards desistance. Given that participation in RJ is voluntary and requires acknowledgment of the basic facts related to the offence, it is likely that offenders who agree to participate in RJ are already on the course towards desistance.

How can the community benefit from restorative practices?

RJ typically stresses the need for the involvement of the community in the response to crime. The underlying idea is that through community involvement in a restorative intervention the offender and victim might feel better supported and assured of access to resources for their reintegration.

Through involvement, the community also gains insight into the causes of crime emerging within their own community and possibly how to counteract them. Dzur and Olson (2004) further argue that mobilisation of the community is sensible since informal community responses and control are more efficient than punishment. As such, RJ aims to contribute to community building and strengthening the community's problem-solving capacity.

Unfortunately, there is little research on what communities want from RJ and how they benefit from it and there is insufficient empirical data on whether communities indeed feel more involved and better equipped to deal with crime through RJ. Also, it is not always clear what community a victim and offender identify with and feel supported by. In these cases, a community of support for the victim and offender must first be revived for community involvement to come about.

References

Daly, K. (2003) 'Mind the gap: restorative justice in theory and practice', in A. von Hirsch, J. Roberts, A.E. Bottoms, K. Roach and M. Schiff (eds) *Restorative justice and criminal justice: competing or reconcilable paradigms?* Oxford: Hart Publishing, pp.219-236.

Dzur, A.W. and Olson, S.M. (2004). The Value of Community Participation in Restorative Justice. *Journal of Social Philosophy*, 35(1), 91-107.

Shapland, J., Robinson, G., & Sorsby, A. (2011). *Restorative justice in practice*. London: Routledge.

Sherman, L.W., & Strang, H. (2007). *Restorative Justice: The Evidence*. London, England: Smith Institute.

Van Camp, T. (2014). *Victims of Violence and Restorative Practices. Finding a voice*. London: Routledge.

Truth and consequences: When crime victims and offenders meet

By <u>Scott Alessi</u> | <u>Print</u> | <u>Share</u>
Article

With U.S. incarceration rates at an unsustainable high, crime victims are taking the lead in an effort to rehabilitate offenders.

Lonnie Jones was just 16 years old when he and a group of friends planned to burglarize an empty home in hopes of making some easy money. They broke into the dark house around 9 p.m. and had nearly completed the robbery when the owner suddenly walked in. As she stood in the doorway and screamed, Jones and his friends panicked. One of the robbers grabbed the woman and another pulled out a knife, stabbing her and leaving her to die as the group fled the scene.

"It was just out of fear," says Jones, looking back on his crime more than three decades later. "I was just a kid. We didn't want to hurt anybody."

Jones was arrested soon after and convicted of murder. Despite his remorse for the terrible consequences of the robbery gone wrong—and being only a minor—he was given a sentence of life in prison plus an additional 109 years. He was then sent to a Texas prison to live out the remainder of his days behind bars.

It was nearly 30 years before Jones, through a coincidental encounter with a former federal judge who pulled some strings on his behalf, was put on a path to parole. He entered a pre-release program in 2007, during which he signed up for a 14-week course called Bridges to Life.

The program, one of a growing number of restorative justice initiatives taking place in prisons around the country, brings together offenders and victims of violent crime in the hope of fostering healing and rehabilitation. In a correctional system struggling to deal with massive overcrowding, budget shortfalls, and high rates of recidivism, restorative justice is offering a new way forward for American prisons.

Bridges to Life was founded by John Sage, whose own life was changed by a crime very similar to the one committed by Jones. In 1993 Sage's sister, Marilyn, was murdered by two teenagers during a burglary. The killers were tried in a Texas court, convicted, and sentenced to death, but even seeing the perpetrators receive the ultimate punishment wasn't enough to console Sage. The loss of his sister sent him on an emotional downward spiral, and nothing in the justice system could help him find solace.

"When you think about the evil of someone killing someone you love, you are kind of staring Satan in the eye," says Sage, a soft-spoken Houston native and lifelong Catholic. "I became a prisoner of all those emotions—anger, revenge, just wanting to hurt somebody. So I was searching for a way to dig out of that hole."

It took Sage nearly five years to work through the trauma of his sister's murder. He was then invited to

participate in a pilot program, developed by Prison Fellowship International, that connected victims and offenders. It proved to be a life-changing experience. The more he learned about restorative justice—which seeks to repair the harm done by crime for all parties involved rather than simply punish the offender—the more Sage felt that such an approach was needed on a larger scale.

Drawing from his personal experience and the pilot program in which he volunteered, Sage developed a curriculum for Bridges to Life. Though it is not intended to convert participants, he says, it does rely heavily on Christian themes such as repentance, reconciliation, and forgiveness.

Inmates and volunteers meet for two-hour sessions that include small group discussions and testimonies from victims, who discuss the ways in which crimes like rape and murder have drastically altered their lives. Participants complete weekly homework assignments and must share their own stories with the group, often taking responsibility for their crimes for the first time.

"It takes [offenders] outside of themselves and shows them what they've done and who they've hurt," says Sage, whose program has now been used in 28 Texas prisons with more than 16,500 inmates completing the course. "We let them talk in a safe place where they can express themselves, express their emotions. This is a counter-culture to the prison."

That approach appealed to Jones, who found the program to be in stark contrast to anything he'd experienced in three decades of living under the supervision of the Texas Department of Corrections.

"Everything in prison is either run by guards or someone from the state, and their first priority is always security. Their first thought is 'This is an inmate,'" he says. "But Bridges to Life, their first priority is getting you to understand what went wrong, where it went wrong, how it affects others, and how it affected you. It just touches a place that other programs in prison, they don't even go there."

Jones completed the program and, still awaiting release, asked if he could enroll a second time. He then participated a third and a fourth time, eventually becoming an honorary teacher and counseling his fellow inmates before finally being granted his release from prison in 2009, 31 years after his arrest.

"That program did for me, and for the other guys I have seen go through it, what nothing else in prison could have done," says Jones, now 50. "There's no way you can just sit there and talk to someone that has been affected by crime, someone that has went through something as traumatic as a rape or a loved one's murder—there's no way you can look them in the eyes and not be affected."

Crime and punishment

The restorative justice movement began in the 1970s in response to what some saw as an alarming trend toward ever more punitive responses to crime. With initiatives such as the "war on drugs," policymakers vowed to be "tough on crime," and the justice system began to emphasize harsh sentencing for even minor offenses as a supposed deterrent to criminal behavior. More offenders were sentenced to longer prison stays, resulting in a system where one in every 104 Americans is now behind bars.

"It seems the rubber band has stretched about as far as it can on a purely punitive philosophy," says Andrew Skotnicki, a religious studies professor at Manhattan College whose books on criminal justice include *The Last Judgment: Christian Ethics in a Legal Culture* (Ashgate). "We still have a very strong retributive philosophy and believe that people go to prison in order to be punished. But at the same time I think we're beginning to question that mentality, because it has produced the most imprisoned people on earth."

According to the latest numbers from the Bureau of Justice Statistics, the United States had 2.3 million citizens in federal, state, or local jails at the end of 2010. (China, with 1.6 million prisoners, is the only country whose inmate population comes close to that of the United States.) The federal and state prison population alone has more than doubled in the last 20 years, growing from 740,000 in 1990 to more than 1.6 million in 2010.

Prison overcrowding has resulted in corrections budgets being stretched to their limits. The average cost of keeping an inmate incarcerated for one year is $29,000, and the Center for Economic and Policy Research reports that federal, state, and local governments combined spent nearly $75 billion on corrections in 2008.

"If for no other reason than economics, we have completely run the penal ship aground," says Skotnicki. "We know it is not working, and we are dying for somebody to give us a good idea that is cost-effective and that ultimately has redemptive effects that change people's lives."

That was the goal for a group of Mennonite researchers who began looking for alternative solutions to criminal justice issues in the mid-1970s. Howard Zehr, who joined the movement in 1978, says that prison overcrowding was already becoming a concern. "But we had no concept of how bad it was really going to get," he says.

Zehr, often called the "grandfather of restorative justice," found that punitive approaches to justice were not truly holding offenders accountable and that the threat of punishment made offenders feel as if they were the victims. Meanwhile the actual victims' needs were being neglected and the community at large was being shut out of the process.

"When I started listening to victims and then seeing what happened when victims and offenders met, it shook up my whole view on justice," says Zehr, a professor of restorative justice at

Eastern Mennonite University in Harrisonburg, Virginia. He came to the conclusion that the traditional questions asked by the justice system—what laws have been broken, who is to blame, and how they should be punished—were not the best approach for the offender, the victim, or the community.

"A fundamental change [with restorative justice] is that we'd be asking different questions," Zehr says. "We would be saying not, 'What punishment does this offender deserve?' but 'How can we resolve this thing in a way that is as healing as possible, as helpful as possible for everybody involved, while holding the offender adequately accountable?' And that's a different question [from the one] we're asking."

Shock to the system

In the last three decades, the new approach pioneered by Zehr has been applied in a number of different ways. In some cases, restorative justice can serve as an alternative method of sentencing, bringing together the offender and their victims to discuss the details of the crime and how best to resolve it, which may or may not result in a prison sentence.

Other programs, like the one developed by Sage, bring inmates into conversation with victims of other crimes—"surrogate victims," as they are sometimes called—providing an opportunity for both parties to heal and preparing inmates for their eventual release. Though restorative justice programs come in many shapes and sizes, they share a similar goal of addressing the consequences of crime in a way that seeks to repair, as best as possible, the harm that has been done.

Janine Geske, a former Wisconsin Supreme Court Justice who now serves as director of the Restorative Justice Initiative at Marquette University, has experimented with a variety of restorative justice models over the past 12 years. She has brought together perpetrators of violent crime and their victims for one-on-one conversations and runs three-day prison workshops that bring together inmates, community members, and crime victims.

These experiences, says Geske, can be transformational for all involved. That doesn't mean, however, that restorative justice guarantees rehabilitation, or even that inmates who participate would not commit another offense if released. "It is more complicated than that," Geske says. "But I do think you can change people's motivation and you can change how people think about [crime]."

At Green Bay Correctional Institution, a maximum security prison in Wisconsin where Geske has been running her program the longest, Warden Michael Baenen says restorative justice programming has deeply affected the institution's climate. Inmates who participate have fewer behavioral problems, he says, making the prison safer. Others have been inspired to suggest community service projects or charity fundraisers they can run from inside the prison. Some have even taken to working in the prison's garden to grow fresh produce for local food pantries.

"Once they can start thinking about the impact of what they do, it just seems to open a gate of being willing to look at different ways of running your life," Baenen says. That's a big help for those who are preparing for reentry into the community, he adds, but it also holds true for those who are never going to be released.

"They are still human beings and they have a positive impact on other people who are going home," Baenen says. "In some cases they are parents and have an impact on their children. So yes, there are definitely benefits."

Tougher on crime

But in a system that has been built on the idea of punishing offenders, not everyone is on board with the concept of restorative justice. "Sometimes I hear law enforcement call it 'hug a thug,'" says Geske.

Critics of the model argue that it is "soft on crime" and goes easy on offenders, which Geske argues couldn't be further from the truth. "This process is harder on them than almost any other program you can give them," she says. "This really calls them to be responsible for victimizing others and having hurt others in ways they never considered."

That's especially true when the offender sits down with the people who were directly affected by their actions. Geske recalls family members showing a murderer a photo of their victim in a casket, or reading to them from the autopsy report. "That is tough stuff for an offender to sit and listen to, which they've never had to do before," she says. "So there is nothing easy about restorative justice."

Sage also encountered some resistance when he began pitching Bridges to Life to prisons. "At first they thought we were nuts," he says with a laugh. Wardens told him that there was no such thing as a confidential meeting in prison, and once they started running the program it was often interrupted by guards. But in time Sage's efforts came to be more accepted by the prison system.

"We had a lot of barriers to overcome in the first few years, and we still do," says Sage. "But I think there's been a lot of work done in Texas and all around the country in people understanding we've got to do something different, and I think the leadership in the prison system in the last 10 years has affected some real attitude changes."

Part of that change is due to the programs' proven success. Nationwide recidivism rates have remained high for the last decade, with a 2011 study by the Pew Center on the States finding that roughly 45 percent of offenders released from state prisons return to the system within three years. But a study of more than 1,000 Bridges to Life graduates released from 14 different prisons between 2005 and 2008 shows a recidivism rate of 18.7 percent, less than half of the national average. "We can't take 100 percent credit (for that number)," admits Sage, "but I know that we are a big piece of the reason."

Many in the prison system have taken notice. Sage's curriculum has been adapted for use in 10 states, and restorative justice programming has been instituted in prisons nationwide. In California, where the prison population peaked in 2006 at 173,000—double the number of inmates the system was built to hold—such programs have been in high demand.

"In different facilities the people at the top are very anxious to have some type of restorative process," says Jesuit Father Michael Kennedy, executive director of the California-based Jesuit Restorative Justice Initiative. Working in prisons ranging from San Quentin down to small juvenile facilities, Kennedy has helped to implement such programs and has seen increasingly positive results among participants.

And since most programs are run by volunteers and supported through donations or underwriters, they come at little or no cost to the state. In a system looking for cost-effective solutions to rehabilitate offenders and cut down on recidivism, economics may be the strongest selling point for restorative justice, says Kennedy. "We wouldn't even be having this conversation if it wasn't for money," he says.

Still, that doesn't mean everyone has jumped on the restorative justice bandwagon. "Are there some people who are totally against it? Of course there are," Kennedy says. "We're always going to have that. But the fact of the matter is, it works."

Second chances

Another common misconception about restorative justice is the belief that it would somehow replace prisons or result in dangerous criminals being released. But proponents of prison reform such as Manhattan College's Skotnicki argue that there are some criminals who absolutely need to be kept behind bars to ensure public safety. Even so, he says, that doesn't mean society should give up on them. Instead, restorative justice advocates argue for a system that focuses more on rehabilitation rather than revenge.

"The fundamental junction between what's wrong with the prison system and what's right with restorative justice goes to respect for the human person," says Scott Wood, director of the Center for Restorative Justice at Loyola Law School in Los Angeles. Wood points to harsh sentencing laws like California's "three strikes" policy, which requires an offender to receive a life sentence upon a third conviction, as a major flaw in the current system. According to the Insight Prison Project, California had more than 3,000 prisoners serving life sentences at the end of 2009 for nonviolent offenses under the three strikes law, though some may have hope of a revised sentence after a 2012 voter referendum authorized changes to the three strikes law.

"To me, what we've done with these sentencing laws is simply thrown people away," Wood says. "Restorative justice on the other side begins with the proposition that every life has worth and great value, so we proceed with a very respectful attitude toward locating the harm that's been done to human relationship through crime and trying to figure out some way to repair that harm or put people back in right relationship."

Finding ways to make amends for the damage his crime caused has now become a top priority for ex-offender Lonnie Jones. "I know it is hard to do. You can't bring back a life," he says. "But I am trying to do the right thing. I know I can't please everybody, but I do what I can."

Jones has been working two jobs, trying to make ends meet and to save for his eventual retirement. He managed to buy a house and met a woman whom he plans to marry this year. But such personal gains are secondary to his efforts to help others. Jones makes time to visit juvenile detention centers to talk to young people about the choices they make and looks for ways to reach out to anyone who might be in need. "That's my way of giving back for what I've done," he says.

Jones credits Bridges to Life with getting him on the right track, as it has done for many other ex-offenders. If it were up to him, he says, the program would be a requirement for every inmate prior to parole.

Restorative justice proponents like Janine Geske share Jones' hope for the future. She continues to work toward larger acceptance of restorative justice practices, including finding new ways to implement them in different situations that might help reduce or even prevent the spread of crime.

"I understand that there are lots of good parts to the criminal justice system, and I certainly wouldn't throw it out," says Geske. "I just think [if we] find ways to have people talk and listen to each other and better understand one another, we're much less likely to hurt each other."

Want to read more? See the web-only sidebars that accompany this article about a mother's struggle with her son's incarceration and restorative justice in New Zealand.

This article appeared in the March 2013 issue of U.S. Catholic *(Vol. 78, No. 3, pages 12-17).*

Western Illinois University
School of Law Enforcement and Justice Administration
LEJA 520 Course Syllabus

Course Information
Course Title: Restorative Justice
Course Number: LEJA 520

Faculty Information
Name: Barry S. McCrary, Ed.D.
Phone Number: 309-298-1220
E-mail: bs-mccrary@wiu.edu

Course Description:

This course reviews the evolution and development of what has come to be known as
Restorative Justice. The learning experience will address a variety of topics including restorative
justice principles, community engagement, victim issues, and restorative practices and change.
This workbook is a collection of various articles for class discussion and research.

Course Learning Outcomes

Upon completion of this course, our graduates will be able to:

1. Demonstrate an understanding of restorative justice concepts, principles, and values.
2. Recognize the traumatic impact of crime on victims, communities, and offenders, and ways to be responsive to the needs and interest of crime victims.
3. Explain the configuration, methods, and potential uses of various restorative practices and evaluate the degree to which they are more or less restorative.
4. Identify several practical strategies for developing active partnerships within the community.
5. Manage personal, interpersonal, and organizational change and prepare strategies for addressing the response to change efforts.
6. Develop the first steps of a plan of action.

Module *Three: Methods, and potential uses of various restorative practices*		
	Details	*Due*
Objectives	**1.1** Compare and contrast the purpose and structure of various restorative justice practices. **1.2** Describe the advantages and disadvantages of community restorative boards, restorative group conferencing and peacemaking circles. **1.3** Identify implementation and operation issues with restorative practices	

RESTORATIVE JUSTICE
IN SCHOOL COMMUNITIES

DAVID R. KARP
BEAU BRESLIN
Skidmore College

In response to recent school violence, most schools in the United States have adopted increasingly punitive disciplinary policies. However, some schools have embraced restorative justice practices. This article explores the recent implementation of these practices in school communities in Minnesota, Colorado, and Pennsylvania, examining how school communities can make use of this approach to address drug and alcohol problems and how this approach may offer an alternative to zero-tolerance policies.

Theorists of the American community argue that socialization, moral integration, and social control operate in the context of social institutions (Bellah, Madsen, Sullivan, Swidler, & Tipton, 1991; Sullivan, 1995). "Strong communities," wrote Philip Selznick (1992), "are institution-centered. Their cohesion and moral competence derive from the strength and integrity of families, schools, parties, government agencies, voluntary associations, and law" (p. 370). With regard to crime, the essential argument derived from social disorganization theory is that institutionally strong communities are better able to prevent crime as well as respond to crime when it happens (Bursik & Grasmick, 1993; Sampson, 1995). Schools as an institution at the societal level and as communities at the micro level are a cornerstone for youth socialization and the social control of delinquent behavior. Restorative and community justice programs in the school setting prioritize activities that try to reduce delinquency and find just solutions to delinquent behavior. Moreover, they try to build

AUTHORS' NOTE: *Address correspondence to David Karp, Department of Sociology, Skidmore College, Saratoga Springs, NY 12866; e-mail: dkarp@skidmore.edu.*

community capacity—to respond to problem behavior without resorting to the criminal justice system and to create a safe and supportive learning environment that effectively expresses the values of the culture (Chavis, 1998; Karp & Clear, 2000).

As a response to juvenile delinquency, the social control practices of two important community institutions—families and schools— need to complement one another. Braithwaite (1989) argued that loving families engage in disciplinary practices that focus on the moral dimension of misbehavior—how the behavior is harmful to oneself or others and the obligation of making amends—and the sanctions families impose are reintegrative. Children may be grounded, but they are not abandoned. The theory behind restorative justice is often associated with Braithwaite's family model of crime control (Bazemore, 1998b; Clear & Karp, 1999; Van Ness & Strong, 1997). When children go to school, they experience a shift to more formal practices of social control, although typically not as impersonal, bureaucratic, and retributive as what they encounter in the justice system. In this article, we examine how the family model of restorative justice is being applied in the school setting. We examine three school-based models, each of which may be characterized by their attempt to strengthen community capacity as they respond to problem behavior.

The focus of this special issue is the relationship between substance abuse treatment and restorative justice. However, the three programs we describe here do not focus specifically on drug and alcohol problems in the school setting (although we focus case examples on such problems). They are comprehensive and often focus on problems of interpersonal conflict. Nevertheless, there are two reasons why these programs are particularly relevant to this special issue.

First, as alluded to earlier, restorative justice programs focus on building community capacity. In this model, drug and alcohol abuse is not merely a problem in its own right but symptomatic of youth alienation, oppositional youth subcultures, and weak community controls. Consequently, restorative practices are not directed simply at curbing drug and alcohol use but changing student culture and strengthening the social ties of youth to conventional people and institutions. This is achieved through comprehensive restorative justice programs rather than ones focusing narrowly on a particular set of disciplinary problems.

Second, although the programs described here are more broadly defined, drug and alcohol use figure prominently in the repertoire of school disciplinary problems. In a 1997 national survey of high school students (Kaufman et al., 2000), 51% had consumed alcohol in the 30 days prior to the survey, and 26% had smoked marijuana. Although most reported that they did not use alcohol or other drugs at school, 32% said that drugs were made available to them on school property. Drug and alcohol use is also a warning sign for other student problem behavior such as poor academic performance and interpersonal conflict (Dwyer, Osher, & Warger, 1998; Gottfredson, 1997). In this article, we examine how three school-based restorative programs respond to drug and alcohol problems and how these responses are located within a larger conceptual framework that seeks to change student culture by strengthening behavioral norms and cultivating individual responsibility.

COMMUNITY CAPACITY AND RELATIONAL REHABILITATION

In a recent analysis, Bazemore (1999) argued that restorative justice practices are implicitly engaged in "relational rehabilitation," which is contrasted with traditional conceptions of rehabilitation. He defined it as an approach that "links crime to a breakdown in social relationships and hence prescribes a reintegrative response to crime focused on attempts to repair, rebuild and enhance bonds or ties between young offenders and their communities" (p. 155). This approach differs from traditional rehabilitation, he argued, for three reasons. First, rather than focus singly on offenders, attention is equally paid to all stakeholders in a criminal event, including the victim and other relevant community members (i.e., the offender's family, school teacher, etc.). Second, rather than based in the clinical work of a counselor/ offender relationship, the basis for offender adjustment is in his or her natural or community relationships that need strengthening. Third, the approach extends beyond the focus of offender needs and obligations to the larger social context, building wherever possible community capacity to deliver opportunities to the offender, such as education, job training, employment, and community service work. In this approach, rehabilitation as an outcome is better understood as reintegration through the strengthening of social ties and social functioning rather than as individual cognitive or emotional adjustment. Bazemore, Dooley, and Nissen (2000) wrote,

> The problem among some advocates of effective treatment, however, has been a failure to acknowledge that rehabilitation is a bigger issue than changing the attitudes, thinking, and problematic behavior of offenders. The question restorative justice might pose then is: What good is an initial change in thinking and behavior patterns if the offender's relationships with law-abiding adults and peers are weak or nonexistent? (p. 18)

School-based restorative justice is characterized by its focus on relational rehabilitation. Contemporary education theory emphasizes that school effectiveness is predicated on community building in the school (Sergiovanni, 1994). Distinguishing a community from an organization, Sergiovanni (1994) argued that relationships between school members (teachers, students, and staff members) are not merely instrumental but have a moral interdependence. "Relationships within a community of mind are based not on contracts but on understandings about what is shared and on the emerging web of obligations to embody that which is shared" (Sergiovanni, 1994, p. 7). Thus, when school rules or the criminal law is broken, harm is defined not in terms of the technical infraction but by the effects on other members of the community. The web of obligations includes the needs of both the victims and the offender as well as the needs of the community to sustain a safe learning culture. Such a school community would be characterized by its social support (Cullen, 1994; Maruna, 2001) rather than its coercive control.

RETRIBUTIVE AND RESTORATIVE PRACTICES

At this stage, restorative justice in the schools is largely an abstract idea. Given recent concerns for school safety, most U.S. schools have adopted retributive, disintegrative disciplinary policies. For the 1996-1997 school year, most public schools (K-12) maintained zero-tolerance policies for alcohol (87%) and other drugs (88%). Forty-five percent of public high schools conducted drug sweeps, and 22% percent of all public schools (K-12) had taken disciplinary actions against students for alcohol or drugs (including tobacco) in that year. This amounts to nearly 21,000 schools taking more than 170,000 disciplinary actions of expulsion, transfer, or out-of-school suspensions of more than 5 days (Kaufman et al., 2000).

What we have seen in the past decade is a retrenchment of school disciplinary policies that are based on authoritative control and greater collaboration between school administrators with private security and local police. School policies emphasize zero tolerance for rule breaking and exclusion of offenders from the school community. In others words, community is built on fear rather than care. Restorative practices, therefore, require a radical shift in philosophy, and the tension between retributive, authoritarian controls and restorative, communitarian controls is a major theme in community justice.

In Australia, where school-based restorative practices emerged in the early 1990s, a similar problem of clashing philosophies has proven problematic for wide-scale implementation. Cameron and Thorsborne (1999) observed,

> While some schools have adopted humane philosophies closely aligned with what we now understand to be a restorative justice philosophy, it would be rare that misconduct is generally viewed from a harm-to-relationships perspective, with decisions about what to do about the incident centering around how to repair the harm. It is more likely that responses to (even low-level) wrongdoing are still driven by a belief that punishment works, and compliance is all about maintenance of control. (p. 5)

Restorative justice requires a shift in philosophy away from authoritarian controls because they effectively deny offenders and victims a meaningful role in the sanctioning process. Without having a participatory role, the resolution is much less likely to become a learning experience for the offender and an opportunity for him or her to develop a sense of personal responsibility. And the needs of the victim as well as the harm to the community are unlikely to be addressed. At their extreme, authoritarian controls in the school can be characterized as coercive, engendering the possibility that delinquency will increase as an oppositional response to perceived oppression. In a general theoretical statement, Colvin (2000) argued, "Coercion produces alienated bonds, which, if reinforced by continual coercive relations, produce chronic involvement in serious delinquent behavior" (p. 16). He went on to write,

> While most students resign themselves to [coercive social control], a significant number of students actively (usually as individuals) resist. Such resistance leads to further coercive controls and ultimately to complete alienation from both the school and external authority in general. While the intended outcome of schools is to create compliant students, the latent outcome is the creation of a number of young people who become more marginalized with even greater social-psychological deficits. (p. 70)

School programs that have been found to be effective responses to drug and alcohol use share the following features, each of which is consistent with restorative approaches to the problem. First, effective school programs articulate clear norms and behavioral standards. Second, they institutionalize competency development by providing long-term programming in such areas as developing self-control, stress management, responsible decision making, social problem solving, and communication skills (Gottfredson, 1997). Unfortunately, the need for restorative practices may be all the more pressing because when schools are not busy suspending and expelling, they often make use of ill-conceived drug and alcohol educational programs. This article explores an alternative approach.

At present, the following three geographical locations represent the collective ideological and pragmatic center of the school-based restorative justice movement in the United States: the statewide school system in Minnesota, 15 schools in the Denver metropolitan area, and a small band of 6 "alternative" facilities located in southeastern Pennsylvania. To be sure, restorative justice practices in various forms and in various settings have surfaced in other pockets of the country. But nowhere is the idea practiced more widely or has the philosophy been bought into more completely than in these three locations. In this article, we describe the restorative practices of these sites. Data were collected from published reports by the schools and telephone interviews with key informants.

Each of the three school-based restorative justice projects emerged from a combination of factors, beginning with a shared sense of concern on the part of teachers and administrators that the growing incidents of school-related violence were disrupting the central mission of the educational community. Recent studies have demonstrated that youth violence steadily increased during the 1980s, reaching its peak in the early 1990s at the precise moment when many school officials were searching for more effective ways to control student misbehavior (Snyder & Sickmund, 1999). Whereas most school administrators believed the solution to ineffective disciplinary policies was to increase the severity of traditional punishments, a few adopted a new philosophical approach.

MINNESOTA PUBLIC SCHOOLS

The genesis of Minnesota's restorative justice project dates back to 1995 when together with the federal government, the state allocated money in an attempt to guide districts and communities in developing effective violence prevention and peacemaking programs. At that time, the Minnesota Department of Children, Families and Learning (the state's department of education) was charged with the responsibility of constructing a 5-year plan to reduce violence throughout the state's public school system. The hope was that stronger communities could be fostered by tackling both the factors contributing to violence among adolescents and perhaps more importantly, the reactions of schools to individual incidents of harm. The original sponsors of the program were troubled by the fact that occasions of school violence were typically managed by institutions outside the school setting that had little tangible connection to the enterprise of teaching itself. Most notably, the state's juvenile justice system was the primary venue for the resolution of major youth conflicts.

Restorative justice advocates were concerned that in most schools, all types of offenses were (and are still) resolved through a structure that allows authority figures—principals, teachers, counselors, and so on—to dictate punishments without much consideration of the victim's feelings or the offender's needs. Based on the retributive model, schools dole out sanctions in line with precedent and with little acknowledgment of the broader communal implications. The focus is not on making amends but is directed at the specific violation of the law. When a harm is done, in other words, there develops a clear separation between the authority figure, the offender, and the community at large; the relationship between offender and the school is described as one way, much like the relationship between the state and the criminal. The victim is marginalized and told that he or she is not important to the process, and the result is often suspension or the removal of the offender from the learning environment. In such instances, the offender likely becomes bitter and antiauthoritarian, the victim becomes dissatisfied because of a lack of closure, and the community loses one of its members.

Accordingly, the state's 5-year plan included the adoption of a restorative philosophy to provide teachers and administrators with an alternative to the more common methods of punishment. The embrace of restorative measures was not directed at replacing traditional means of discipline but to provide an additional resource for schools to handle their own internal problems. A follow-up to the original 5-year plan noted that "by applying restorative measures in schools, school personnel have another tool to use with children and youth to repair harm and teach problem solving skills" (Minnesota Department of Children, Families and Learning, 1996, p. 3). Administrative personnel, teachers, and members of the community at large (corrections officers, interested citizens, etc.) are trained in restorative conferencing techniques and are asked to use the skills gained both as a means and an end. One of the common techniques used are circles that bring together victims, offenders, supporters of each, and other community members to discuss the effect of the offense, find strategies for repairing the harm and reintegrating the offender, and build community. For a comparison of the major restorative models, including circles, see Bazemore (1998a).

Currently, almost half the school districts in Minnesota are making some use of restorative practices, and four districts are using them extensively. These four districts each received a share of a $300,000 appropriation from the Minnesota State Legislature to evaluate "alternative approaches" to school discipline problems (Minnesota Department of Children, Families and Learning, 2000). In particular, the districts developed strategies for combating common rule violations that resulted in suspensions and expulsions by infusing restorative justice measures into the school's internal judicial or disciplinary structures. Beginning in 1998, the goal of the 3-year project has been to evaluate the effect restorative measures have in both the classroom and the larger educational community. Although the evaluation remains incomplete at this time, we refer here to evaluation information currently available.

The preliminary numbers from this study are intriguing. In the Minneapolis school district, the Seward Montessori Elementary School witnessed a 27% reduction in the number of suspensions and expulsions during the first year of the project. Similarly, the Kaposia and Lincoln Center elementary schools observed an equally dramatic drop in the number of disciplinary actions. Lincoln Center Elementary School, which has data from 1997, has seen the number of referrals for violent behavior decrease by more than half. After 2 years of restorative practices, the number of reports of violence decreased from seven per day to less than two. Such progress is impressive, particularly in light of the fact that the school district implemented a new policy requiring teachers to report all violent activity to school authorities. The numbers emerging from the Kaposia Elementary School reflect similar trends.

What is most interesting is that the two high schools participating in the study—Princeton High School and South St. Paul High School—also saw dramatic reductions in major disciplinary action. At Princeton High, officials noted that there was a simultaneous reduction in the number of detentions and the number of out-of-school suspensions. The same is true of South St. Paul High, where administrators imposed 110 out-of-school suspension days in the first year of the program but only 65 in the second. Nancy Riestenberg, violence prevention specialist at the Minnesota Department of Children, Families and Learning, admitted that a percentage of the reduction may be due to a number of structural variables, including the fact that the existence of state funds has no doubt influenced school administrators to comply with the study. But she also suggested that creating additional options for disciplinary action—options that seek to reintegrate offenders and restore victims rather than simply separating them and punishing the former—has allowed school administrators the freedom to construct creative remedies. Such freedom, she contended, does in fact contribute to deterrence and reduced levels of recidivism.

The four Minnesota districts that have thus far embraced restorative justice as an alternative means of control are no different than traditional schools in terms of the prevalence of drugs and alcohol among the student population. What is different is the schools' response to these ubiquitous problems. Where traditional schools immediately turn hard-core offenders—particularly repeat offenders—over to the juvenile justice system, schools that employ restorative justice seek to reintegrate offenders back into the community by educating them about the effect of their individual actions. And this is particularly true with regard to drug and alcohol use. The belief that possession and use constitutes a victimless crime is antithetical to the principle of restorative justice where at the very least, a harm is done to the community every time a student comes to school under the influence.

To help anticipate these and similar problems, officials at the Minnesota Department of Children, Families and Learning have identified chemical health coordinators within individual schools as the most obvious targets for restorative justice training. At the four demonstration sites already in operation, the chemical health coordinator participates in restorative conferences when the harm involves the use of drugs or alcohol. This policy is meant to minimize any potential liability that may accompany a sensitive and delicate issue as well as to provide the group with an expert trained in the field of drug and alcohol abuse. Indeed, the educational approach to dealing with major issues such as alcohol and drug use has always been one of caution.

Mary Ticiu, assistant principal at Stillwater High School, described a recent case in which a teenager was suspected of using marijuana on school grounds. The school's initial response to these particular accounts of drug use was to approach the young woman and inquire as to the accuracy of such reports. The woman apparently was not altogether forthcoming at the beginning of the process, and thus school officials had further reason to suspect that the rumors of her marijuana use were in fact true. At that point, administrators asked the student whether she would agree to an informal search, from which a small stash of rolling papers was discovered. No illegal substances were found on the student. Ticiu noted that this provided an ideal scenario for the inclusion of restorative justice in the case.

A restorative conference was organized with the offender, those that were described as her suppliers, the chemical health specialist at the school, affected members of the student body, and some members of the faculty and staff. The goal, Ticiu noted, was not to punish the young woman or to create a police state in which students' rights and privacy would be threatened but rather was to create an environment for all the major stakeholders to learn from each other. The offending student was first permitted to tell her story, to articulate to the entire community the reasons for her actions. She also took the opportunity, Ticiu remarked, to seek forgiveness from those around her. All the additional members of the conference were then permitted to raise issues and concerns relevant to their relationship with the offender. The end result was that the student was made aware of the effect of her actions and thus agreed to periodic checks to monitor her continued sobriety.

Ticiu noted that such cases are rare. Drug and alcohol cases within the schools are not altogether common, she says, and those situations that do surface are often handled outside the academic setting. Sometimes, she argued, the seriousness of the drug and/or alcohol abuse warrants action from officials in the juvenile justice system. Other times, the offender may choose to go outside the school to seek some kind of resolution. In cases involving low-level drug and alcohol use (similar to the aforementioned case), a student will most likely have the option of staying within the disciplinary structure of the school—and thus participating in a restorative justice meeting—or taking his or her chances within the traditional juvenile justice system. Ticiu noted that a fair number—close to 50%—choose the more traditional route. She speculated that they make this choice primarily because they are less knowledgeable about restorative practices and prefer traditional punishment because it is a known quantity.

DENVER METROPOLITAN SCHOOLS

In 1997, the Colorado School Mediation Project (CSMP), a nonprofit organization devoted to the principles of conflict management, identified 15 schools in the Denver metropolitan area as potentially receptive to the idea of implementing restorative measures into their disciplinary systems. Most of the schools in the ongoing pilot project are elementary and middle schools, but a few are secondary schools. The core question addressed has been: What would the addition of restorative justice practices do to improve the well-being of the community?

According to David Claassen-Wilson, restorative justice cocoordinator at CSMP, schools are ideal communities for restorative practices. The educational mission of a school aligns well with the core principles of restorative justice, which emphasize conversation and dialogue. An interchange between the major stakeholders in a given community is at its most basic an exercise in learning, he said. It is an inquiry into the nature of relationships, group dynamics, and the understanding of the self. Indeed, one learns about the effect of an offense when the victim, interested members of the community, and the offender all share their feelings, concerns, and reactions. Thus, the restorative ethos, Claassen-Wilson insisted, is merely an extension of the entire educational enterprise.

Depending on the particular school and the specifics of the case, a variety of formats are used in Colorado to resolve differences. They tend to range from the more informal classroom meetings where the teacher calls an impromptu circle to address a student's misbehavior to the more formal victim impact panels where student offenders learn about the effects of their type of offense from victims of similar offenses. Victim impact panels and more formal conferencing are favored when the case involves a higher degree of severity. Possession of drugs, vandalism, theft, assaults, and harassment are characteristic of offenses that warrant a more formal approach.

A typical conference, Claassen-Wilson explained, begins with the offender telling his or her side of the story. The victim, who recounts his or her memory of the events, then follows the initial contribution by the offender. At that point, supporters (family members, friends, etc.) of both the offender and the victim have an opportunity to address the group and discuss how they were affected. Finally, school administrators offer their perspective on the event. After everyone has had a chance to speak, all participants, including the two major stakeholders, discuss possible solutions. The goal is for the offender to take responsibility for the harm and make amends to those who have been injured. An agreement or contract is then drafted, and the offender is both expected to sign the contract and fulfill its various conditions.

Along the continuum of possible responses, alcohol and drug use obviously demands a more formal approach. Claassen-Wilson noted that their possession and use in the schools raise complicated issues from a restorative justice perspective. They are on the one hand illegal and thus require the intervention of the police. But on the other hand, restorative justice practices can be quite helpful in demonstrating to the offender how his or her actions have affected the community. Often it is that intimate connection to the community that induces an offender to claim responsibility for his or her actions. One of the main components of a successful restorative justice program, Claassen-Wilson argued, is that it encourages greater accountability on the part of the offender.

CSMP therefore recommends a loose combination of restorative justice and traditional punitive responses when dealing with the more severe criminal offenses. Typically, when a student is caught selling drugs, the authorities are called in and the student is expelled. After reentry back into the school, however, restorative justice techniques can be an effective tool in helping prevent a recurrence of the original behavior. Proponents suggest, in other words, that an offender can learn how his or her activities affected the community even after he or she has moved through the juvenile justice system. Here, however, the focus of the conversation changes from one based on restoration and making amends to one that is primarily relational. In other words, a conference that takes place at reentry will likely focus on questions regarding the safety and health of the offender as well as the community rather than on the original offense itself.

The frustration for most advocates of the restorative justice philosophy when considering examples of drug and alcohol use is that by default, restorative measures remain subordinate to the more punitive-oriented juvenile justice system. Even when the state enters into an agreement with the school and thus defers to the school's internal judicial system, the state still retains primary authority. That is to say, because of the illegal nature of the offense, restorative justice practices must give way to the interests of the state. The possession, use, and distribution of illegal substances cannot be tolerated, and thus traditional forms of punishment are the first lines of defense for most schools. The difficulty in conceding such a reality is that the restorative and punitive models are based largely on incompatible paradigms. A punitive system is centered on the notion of retribution, whereas the foundation of the restorative model, in the words of official CSMP documents, should be viewed as "a re-definition of crime as injury to the victim and the community rather than an affront to the power of authorities" (Colorado School Mediation Project, 2000, p. 2). Combining the two responses within the single arena of drug and alcohol use requires some accommodation of the school to the larger claims of the state.

David Hines of the Woodbury Police Department in Woodbury, Minnesota, captured the essence of this frustration most accurately when he remarked that traditional forms of discipline, whether they be for common misbehavior or the most serious harms, are not meeting the needs of the community. Suspension and dismissal, he suggested, run counter to the mission of the entire educational system because they remove the offender from the environment, thereby not allowing the community of educators to do what it does best. In addition, informal studies have revealed that certain students are not deterred from engaging in misbehavior because suspension or removal from school is an attractive option. Many delinquent students, in other words, want to be suspended. Hines thus argued that standard responses to misbehavior can be more detrimental to the overall effectiveness of the school.

BUXMONT ACADEMY

High schools typically are more resistant than elementary and middle schools to substantial philosophical and pedagogical changes. The experience of older students (and/or their parents) can contribute to a conservative mentality whereby the entire community, set in its ways, prefers the status quo. Introducing a philosophical change of the magnitude proposed by restorative justice supporters, therefore, is often met with comparatively high resistance in the high school setting. In addition, elementary schools are also more receptive to the general practice of restorative justice because of the organizational structure of American schools more generally. In secondary schools, a teacher may see a student for at most approximately 1 hour per day, whereas an elementary school teacher has the benefit of constant and continual interaction with the same group of students. Bonds are thus formed in the elementary schools that are more difficult to cultivate within the high school setting.

It is perhaps all the more surprising that restorative practices have been implemented so seamlessly in six alternative schools in Southeastern Pennsylvania. There, the entire student body falls into the 12- to 18-year-old range. Community Service Foundation (CSF) is the parent organization of Buxmont Academy, the collective name for these alternative schools, located in the communities of Bethlehem, Feasterville, Lansdale, Sellersville, Trevose, and Upper Providence. Founded in 1977 by two Pennsylvania educators, Ted and Susan Wachtel, CSF oversees the operation of Buxmont Academy as well as the academy's sister organization, Real Justice, an international training and advocacy group that promotes restorative practices as a novel way of responding to crime and wrongdoing. The outgrowth of the intersection of these various organizations—CSF, Buxmont Academy, and Real Justice—is a school system that advocates alternatives to traditional conflict resolution and champions the principles of restorative justice.

The students attending Buxmont Academy are all "troubled" or "at-risk" youth referred by their public high schools to one of the locations because they have demonstrated one or more of the most common behavioral or emotional problems. Many are on probation and have encountered the juvenile justice system in a variety of ways. Typical problems may include legal difficulties; dysfunctional family situations; aggressive behavioral problems; sexual, physical, or emotional abuse; and mental health impediments. Far more frequently, however, Buxmont Academy teachers and counselors educate students who have had drug and alcohol problems in their home schools. Indeed, the institution devotes a significant portion of its resources to aftercare programs. Much of the energy of the place is directed at providing a haven for young men and women leaving residential drug and alcohol treatment facilities so that they can successfully reintegrate back into more normal social and educational environments.

Bob Costello, assistant director of Real Justice and former director of the Bethlehem site, describes the six satellites of the Buxmont Academy as combining the components of a traditional academic school with the services of a day treatment program. The facilities are licensed by the State Departments of Public Welfare and Public Health as day treatment programs; the only significant difference between Buxmont Academy and other programs that aim to resolve juvenile drug and alcohol problems is that the former places an equal emphasis on education. Costello thus suggested that Buxmont Academy should be viewed by outsiders primarily as a hybrid of the two important institutions. It is not exactly a traditional school, he argued, but neither is it exactly a recovery treatment center; it combines elements of both. Indeed, the six sites act as micro communities into which students can find a place to reintegrate, both educationally and socially, before returning to schools in their home districts.

The restorative justice philosophy, as it has been applied to Buxmont Academy, was described most accurately by Wachtel (2001):

> Our society's fundamental assumption is that punishment holds offenders accountable. However, for an offending student punishment is a passive experience, demanding little or no participation. While the teacher or administrator scolds, lectures and imposes the punishment, the student remains silent, resents the authority figure, feels angry and perceives himself as the victim. The student does not think about the real victims of his offense or the other individuals who have been adversely affected by his actions.

Accountability for Wachtel is more than just taking responsibility for one's actions. It also involves active participation in the process of adjudicating disputes. Resolving problems, in other words, is an ongoing enterprise where all parties share in the discussion and the ultimate resolution. This, obviously, is where the principles of restorative justice surface. Restorative practices allow students to take responsibility for their decisions without making them passive observers in the process.

For the entire disciplinary system to work, Wachtel (2001) insisted, the schools must do their part. The specific philosophy that informs much of Buxmont Academy is loosely borrowed from Braithwaite (1989) and Baumrind (1996), who independently argued that the family model of social control is largely at odds with the more punitive style that pervades many of our contemporary institutions. Indeed, Baumrind argued that the disciplinary style of a parent is importantly distinct from that outside the home in that a child may be reprimanded for wrongdoing by a family member but is then not banished or abandoned from the family altogether (Brower, 1989). There is usually no question that a child will be reintegrated back into the family unit. Restoration, therefore, is a critical component of the informal disciplinary structure that pervades the modern family.

Baumrind further suggested that reconciling the different paradigms of social control may result in widespread benefits to all (Brower, 1989). Buxmont Academy has adopted this view, insisting that schools can be more productive and more effective in controlling misbehavior if they adopt some of the core principles of the family model. To that end, Wachtel (2001) proposed showing "disapproval of [the] wrongdoing, while [simultaneously] supporting and valuing the intrinsic worth of the student who has committed the wrong." High control combined with high support is their approach to introducing a family model into the school systems. Wrongdoing by students, Wachtel said, is not to be tolerated but neither is a standard response by school administrators that does not recognize the capacity of young men and women to respond positively to adversity. Buxmont Academy rests most profoundly on this fundamental principle.

Paul McCold, a criminologist who works closely with Real Justice, noted that the use or possession of illegal substances on school grounds most often results in the immediate notification of the local or state police. At a minimum, juveniles on probation will be required to meet with their probation officers if they are caught with illegal substances. School authorities around the country, McCold said, have some discretion depending on the particular situation, yet possession of an illegal substance more often than not warrants the inclusion of public authorities. Thus, all of the schools must negotiate a path between internal restorative practices and the more dominant retributive approach the students will likely encounter in the juvenile court. They work in complement, however, when high social control is combined with strong social support.

A student who has been caught with drugs or alcohol at one of the Buxmont sites has the opportunity to make amends to the community. He or she will have to face his or her peers and explain the circumstances surrounding the event. An offender who goes exclusively through the juvenile justice system will not have those same opportunities. It is unlikely that he or she will have the chance to learn from his or her colleagues and peers about the personal and collective effect of his or her actions. The juvenile justice system, according to officials at Real Justice, simply does not subscribe to a philosophy that promotes high levels of support.

On one level, drug and alcohol use at Buxmont Academy is handled in a similar fashion to the other sites. Conferencing will be used to bring offenders before the affected community to repair the harm and rebuild fractured relationships. Yet because Buxmont is fundamentally a treatment program, restorative justice practices are embedded in the daily activities of educational learning and group therapy. Discussion of the effect of drug abuse, for example, is not limited to a particular conference in response to a particular offense but is likely to take place in a more informal talking circle. The basic focus of restorative justice—that drug and alcohol abuse is dangerous not only to oneself but to close others and the community as a whole—is a recurring theme in Buxmont's treatment paradigm. Behavioral change based on the principle of relational rehabilitation (Bazemore, 1999) occurs because offenders are given the opportunity to learn about the consequences of their actions and take steps to redefine their place in the larger community.

CONCLUSION

Despite their common interests, there has been very little coordination between the three sites discussed here. Yet the three major centers share a common philosophy, a commitment to the idea that restoration is a more appropriate educational tool than traditional punitive measures for handling harms done to both individuals and communities. Some practices and interests notably diverge, however.

Differences begin with language. None of the three centers share the same title for their restorative experiences, and only one—the Denver program—even uses the word *justice* in the title. In Minnesota, restorative justice practices in the schools are referred to as *restorative measures*. Riestenberg remarked that the name change was adopted consciously so as to draw a clear distinction between the restorative activities undertaken in the schools and the juvenile justice system itself. In contrast, Buxmont Academy administrators take a more ideological approach, suggesting that their embrace of the term *restorative practices* rather than *restorative justice* is related to their shared belief that the concept of justice is elusive and virtually unattainable. To assume that whatever mechanisms available would result in the realization of justice—whether they are punitive or restorative in nature—would, according to officials at Buxmont Academy and Real Justice, be presumptuous.

Another difference lies in the schools' varying commitments to the philosophy of restorative justice. In traditional school settings, such as those in Denver and Minnesota, restorative practices are used primarily as a formal way of resolving differences. A child misbehaves, for example, and a community group conference or circle is organized in response to that misbehavior. Note, however, that there is typically a clear separation between the event and the attempt at restoration. That separation likely results in a few days elapsing before the facilitator can convene a restorative meeting. The deliberative nature of conferencing or circle sentencing often precludes the possibility of resolving problems immediately. Spokespersons for both organizations noted that certain teachers and administrators employ restorative practices informally but that a majority of school personnel are largely unfamiliar with the philosophy of restoration. In Minnesota's Seward Montessori School, for example, only 18 teachers, administrators, and aides were trained in 1999. The entire staff "received an overview presentation of the circle process at the beginning of the [1999-2000] school year" (Minnesota Department of Children, Families and Learning, 2001, p. 1), but that does not mean that they are prepared to adopt restorative measures in all settings. To be sure, certain teachers at Seward and other Minnesota schools have taken the restorative philosophy to a different level by using circles and other forms of conflict resolution as a way to offset any potential problems. And the same is true in Denver. Some teachers in both locations are conferencing with their classes at the opening of every school day so as to prevent future misbehavior. But generally, restorative practices in more traditional educational settings act as an alternative form of conflict resolution and not necessarily as a broader, more comprehensive presence. Indeed, most teachers and administrators at these schools still adhere to traditional disciplinary paradigms.

This is all in contrast to Buxmont Academy where every teacher/ counselor is trained in the practices of restorative justice. Observers of the various Buxmont sites have often commented that there is restorative justice going on all day, in every classroom, involving virtually every relationship. Perhaps because of the mission of these academic institutions—a mission that includes not just education but also rehabilitation and support—the principles of restoration and reintegration are more central. Group sessions are arguably the most critical aspect of the Buxmont experience, and they are modeled on the restorative justice ideal. They are also the primary venue for the community's ongoing dialogue about the implications of substance abuse. Discussions about harm, making amends, and taking responsibility for one's actions—including those related to illegal substances—are a necessary part of the process of enabling at-risk youth to become whole again, noted Costello. Teachers and administrators, therefore, are more likely than in other academic settings to handle minor offenses as well as major offenses in a restorative manner.

The findings from our examination of restorative justice in the school setting disclose both commonalities and differences between the three cases. Certainly, our data cannot provide evidence regarding the effectiveness of the restorative approach either between one another or in contrast to traditional disciplinary measures. Rather, the purpose has been exploratory—what does the school-based approach look like in practice?

What we have discovered is that these sites draw no particular distinction between substance abuse problems and other types of offenses. The approach is seen as applicable to any situation involving harm to oneself or others in a community setting. The common approach, whether applied by conferencing or circles, is to create a collective opportunity to reflect on the behavior and its consequences, seeking a resolution that repairs harm and reconnects marginalized stakeholders. The solution is determined collectively and can vary dramatically depending on circumstances, needs, and desires of those involved. At its best, the restorative approach transforms a student violation into an opportunity for learning—learning about the harm of the offense, learning about the responsibilities of community membership, and learning about democratic decision making and participation.

Three areas stand out as especially problematic for implementation. Restorative justice programs simply take a lot of time, particularly in contrast to traditional sanctions. Restorative justice programs face resistance from the outside, for example, from school district superintendents and juvenile justice professionals. And these programs face resistance from within; this new philosophy is difficult to fully grasp and embrace.

First, school administrators are concerned about the time needed to (a) train facilitators, (b) see a meaningful change in the school's attitude toward punishment (typically 1 to 3 years), and (c) repair specific harms. In the past, the typical school response was swift and decisive: If the harm were significant enough, the child would automatically face suspension. Yet with the use of circles and conferences and because the core philosophy has changed so dramatically, swift action is sacrificed in favor of community-wide debate and contemplation.

Second, each of the programs has an awkward relationship with broader institutional policies that are grounded in retributive justice. In no consistent way do they reconcile an inevitable philosophical tension. They either develop arbitrary policies that distinguish what kinds of offenses can be diverted to the restorative justice practices, coexist by having students proceed through both systems simultaneously, or seek to implement restorative practices after the punitive processes have done their work. Umbreit (1999) speculated that restorative justice programs are particularly vulnerable to co-optation unless clear standards can be articulated.

The final area that remains problematic is not external co-optation but internal inertia. Every principal, teacher, counselor, and student has been socialized in a culture of retribution, and its language, even veneration, permeates all sanctioning processes. Even when restorative practices are fully adopted, it is hard to accept them without suspicion. Where a partial staff implements the practices and where training, even for them, is not comprehensive, we can expect the tension between retribution and restoration to be a significant obstacle.

In each of these case studies, restorative justice approaches are taken to address school disciplinary problems. Although drug and alcohol use are pervasive among youth, these programs have not developed specific responses to these problems except insofar as they require intervention by the juvenile justice system. Nevertheless, what is distinctive about their approach is the location of intervention within the context of the school environment. Rather than exclude the student or "treat" the student in isolation from his or her social world, the response is embedded in the student's community. This approach, therefore, enjoins the student to consider the consequences of the misbehavior on himself or herself and others. It also creates the opportunity for the student to reevaluate and rebuild his or her social ties. Perhaps most important with regard to drug and alcohol use, the restorative approach seeks to change student culture by confronting the behavior in the context of student life and helping students to identify compelling alternatives.

REFERENCES

Baumrind, D. (1996). The discipline controversy revisited. *Family Relations, 45*, 405-505.

Bazemore, G. (1998a). The "community" in community justice: Issues, themes, and questions for the new neighborhood sanctioning models. In D. R. Karp (Ed.), *Community justice: An emerging field* (pp. 327-372). Lanham, MD: Rowman and Littlefield.

Bazemore, G. (1998b). Restorative justice and earned redemption. *American Behavioral Scientist, 41*, 768-813.

Bazemore, G. (1999). After shaming, whither reintegration: Restorative justice and relational rehabilitation. In G. Bazemore & L. Walgrave (Eds.), *Restorative juvenile justice* (pp. 155-194). Monsey, NY: Criminal Justice Press.

Bazemore, G., Dooley, M., & Nissen, L. (2000). Mobilizing social support and building relationships: Broadening correctional and rehabilitative agendas. *Corrections Management Quarterly, 4*, 10-21.

Bellah, R. N., Madsen, R., Sullivan, W. M., Swidler, A., & Tipton, S. M. (1991). *The good society*. Berkeley: University of California Press.

Braithwaite, J. (1989). *Crime, shame, and reintegration*. Cambridge, UK: Cambridge University Press.

Brower, B. (1989). Teenagers reap broad benefits from authoritative parents. *Science News, 136*(8), 117-118.

Bursik, R. J., & Grasmick, H. G. (1993). *Neighborhoods and crime: The dimensions of effective community control*. Lexington, MA: Lexington Books.

Cameron, L., & Thorsborne, M. (1999). *Restorative justice and school discipline: mutually exclusive? A practitioner's view of the impact of community conferencing in Queensland schools* [Online]. Available: http://www.realjustice.org/Pages/schooldisc.html

Chavis, D. (1998). Building community capacity to prevent violence through coalitions and partnerships. In D. R. Karp (Ed.), *Community justice: An emerging field* (pp. 81-94). Lanham, MD: Rowman and Littlefield.

Clear, T. R., & Karp, D. R. (1999). *The community justice ideal.* Boulder, CO: Westview.

Colorado School Mediation Project. (2000). *Restorative justice for schools: A guide to understanding the principles and practices of school-based restorative justice.* Boulder, CO: Author.

Colvin, M. (2000). *Crime and coercion.* New York: St. Martin's.

Cullen, F. T. (1994). Social support as an organizing concept for criminology: Presidential address to the Academy of Criminal Justice Sciences. *Justice Quarterly, 11,* 527-559.

Dwyer, K., Osher, D., & Warger, C. (1998). *Early warning, timely response: A guide to safe schools.* Washington, DC: Department of Education.

Gottfredson, D. (1997). School-based crime prevention. In L. W. Sherman, D. Gottfredson, D. MacKenzie, J. Eck, P. Reuter, & S. Bushway (Eds.), *Preventing crime: What works, what doesn't, what's promising: A report to the United States Congress.* College Park: University of Maryland.

Karp, D. R., & Clear, T. R. (2000). Community justice: A conceptual framework. In *Boundaries changes in criminal justice organizations* (Vol. 2, pp. 323-368). Washington, DC: National Institute of Justice.

Kaufman, P., Chen, X., Choy, S. P., Ruddy, S. A., Miller, A. K., Fleury, J. K., Chandler, K. A., Rand, M. R., Klaus, P., & Planty, M. G. (2000). *Indicators of school crime and safety, 2000* (NCES 2001-017/NCJ-184176). Washington, DC: Departments of Education and Justice.

Maruna, S. (2001). *Making good: How ex-convicts reform and rebuild their lives.* Washington, DC: American Psychological Association.

Minnesota Department of Children, Families and Learning. (1996). *Respecting everyone's ability to resolve problems: Restorative measures.* Roseville, MN: Author.

Minnesota Department of Children, Families and Learning. (2000). *In-school behavior intervention grants: Year 2 evaluation summary* (Draft). Unpublished manuscript.

Minnesota Department of Children, Families and Learning. (2001). In-school behavior intervention grants: 1998-2001 (Draft). Unpublished manuscript.

Sampson, R. J. (1995). The community. In J. Q. Wilson & J. Petersilia (Eds.), *Crime* (pp. 193-216). San Francisco: Institute for Contemporary Studies.

Selznick, P. (1992). *The moral commonwealth.* Berkeley: University of California Press.

Sergiovanni, T. J. (1994). *Building community in schools.* San Francisco: Jossey-Bass.

Snyder, H., & Sickmund, M. (1999). *Juvenile offenders and victims: 1999 national report.* Washington, DC: Office of Juvenile Justice and Delinquency Prevention.

Sullivan, W. M. (1995). Institutions as the infrastructure of democracy. In A. Etzioni (Ed.), *New communitarian thinking* (pp. 170-180). Charlottesville: University of Virginia.

Umbreit, M. S. (1999). Avoiding the marginalization and "McDonaldization" of victim-offender mediation: A case study in moving toward the mainstream. In G. Bazemore & L. Walgrave (Eds.), *Restorative juvenile justice* (pp. 213-234). Monsey, NY: Criminal Justice Press.

Van Ness, D., & Strong, K. H. (1997). *Restoring justice.* Cincinnati, OH: Anderson.

Wachtel, T. (2001). *Safer Saner Schools: Restoring community in a disconnected world* [Online]. Available: http://www.safersanerschools.org/Pages/restorativepractices.html

David Karp, Ph.D., is an assistant professor of sociology at Skidmore College in Saratoga Springs, New York, where he teaches courses in criminology and criminal justice. He conducts research on community-based responses to crime and has given workshops on restorative justice and community justice nationally. Currently, he is engaged *in a qualitative research study examining Vermont's community reparative probation boards and is a member of the New York State Community Justice Forum. He is the author of numerous academic articles and technical reports and two books—*Community Justice: An Emerging Field *and* The Community Justice Ideal *(with Todd Clear).*

Beau Breslin, Ph.D., is an assistant professor of government at Skidmore College. He teaches courses on constitutional law, judicial process, and civil liberties. His research interests include constitutional theory and the interplay between the First Amendment right to free speech and the country's most valued social and political institutions. He is currently completing a manuscript titled The Unconstituted Community: Communitarianism and the Problem of Constitutional Theory.

Western Illinois University
School of Law Enforcement and Justice Administration
LEJA 520 Course Syllabus

Course Information
Course Title: Restorative Justice
Course Number: LEJA 520

Faculty Information
Name: Barry S. McCrary, Ed.D.
Phone Number: 309-298-1220
E-mail: bs-mccrary@wiu.edu

Course Description:

This course reviews the evolution and development of what has come to be known as Restorative Justice. The learning experience will address a variety of topics including restorative justice principles, community engagement, victim issues, and restorative practices and change. This workbook is a collection of various articles for class discussion and research.

Upon completion of this course, our graduates will be able to:

1. Demonstrate an understanding of restorative justice concepts, principles, and values.
2. Recognize the traumatic impact of crime on victims, communities, and offenders, and ways to be responsive to the needs and interest of crime victims.
3. Explain the configuration, methods, and potential uses of various restorative practices and evaluate the degree to which they are more or less restorative.
4. Identify several practical strategies for developing active partnerships within the community.
5. Manage personal, interpersonal, and organizational change and prepare strategies for addressing the response to change efforts.
6. Develop the first steps of a plan of action.

Module *Four: Strategies for developing active partnerships within the community*

	Details
Objectives	**1.1** Discover the meaning and defining features of community. **1.2** Described the importance of community involvement in restorative efforts. **1.3** Describe the impact of culture diversity on community building. **1.4** Determine ways in which partnerships between the criminal justice system and the community can be built.

Western Illinois University
School of Law Enforcement and Justice Administration
LEJA 520 Course Syllabus

Course Information
Course Title: Restorative Justice
Course Number: LEJA 520

Faculty Information
Name: Barry S. McCrary, Ed.D.
Phone Number: 309-298-1220
E-mail: bs-mccrary@wiu.edu

Course Description:

This course reviews the evolution and development of what has come to be known as Restorative Justice. The learning experience will address a variety of topics including restorative justice principles, community engagement, victim issues, and restorative practices and change. This workbook is a collection of various articles for class discussion and research.

Course Learning Outcomes

Upon completion of this course, our graduates will be able to:

1. Demonstrate an understanding of restorative justice concepts, principles, and values.
2. Recognize the traumatic impact of crime on victims, communities, and offenders, and ways to be responsive to the needs and interest of crime victims.
3. Explain the configuration, methods, and potential uses of various restorative practices and evaluate the degree to which they are more or less restorative.
4. Identify several practical strategies for developing active partnerships within the community.
5. Manage personal, interpersonal, and organizational change and prepare strategies for addressing the response to change efforts.
6. Develop the first steps of a plan of action.

Module *Five: Prepare strategies for addressing the response to change efforts.*	
	Details
Objectives	**1.1** Explain the impact of change on individuals, groups and organizations, and common responses when confronted with change. **1.2** Describe why it is important to consider the pace of change, organizational culture, and assumptions surrounding organizational change. When planning a change. **1.3** Explain the Concerns Based Approach, and it use as a practical tool in managing a change effort. **1.4** Assess their system's readiness for restorative change, and devise strategies for movement.

U.S. Department of Justice
National Institute of Corrections

Achieving Performance Excellence (APEX)
Guidebook Series

A practical guide to organizational assessment,
performance improvement, and change management

Culture and
Change
Management:
Using APEX To Facilitate
Organizational Change

U.S. Department of Justice
National Institute of Corrections
320 First Street, NW
Washington, DC 20534

Morris L. Thigpen
Director

Thomas J. Beauclair
Deputy Director

Sherry Carroll
Project Manager

National Institute of Corrections
www.nicic.gov

Achieving Performance Excellence (APEX)
Guidebook Series

A practical guide to organizational assessment,
performance improvement, and change management

Culture and Change Management:
Using APEX To Facilitate Organizational Change

Nancy Cebula
Elizabeth Craig
Christopher Innes, PhD
Theresa Lantz
Tanya Rhone
Tom Ward

People in Charge LLC

NIC Accession No. 025300

April 2012

This manual was developed under cooperative agreement award 11AD01GKF8 from the National Institute of Corrections, U.S. Department of Justice. Points of view or opinions in this document are those of the authors and do not necessarily represent the official opinion or policies of the U.S. Department of Justice.

Suggested Citation: Cebula, Nancy, Elizabeth Craig, Christopher Innes, PhD, Theresa Lantz, Tanya Rhone, and Tom Ward. 2012. *Culture and Change Management: Using APEX To Facilitate Organizational Change*. Washington, DC: U.S. Department of Justice, National Institute of Corrections.

Contents

Foreword

The word "culture" brings to mind the shared beliefs, assumptions, values, attitudes, norms, and practices of the correctional agency. Because culture bears heavily on whether operations and outcomes are in harmony with an agency's mission and goals, culture and change management are critical factors in determining organizational performance.

This segment of the APEX (Achieving Performance Excellence) Guidebook series introduces the fundamentals of organizational culture and provides guidance and assessment tools to help agencies develop strategies to improve organizational performance. When a culture conflicts with an organization's professed mission, vision, and values, the agency is challenged until it faces the complex task of *deliberately* changing its culture. The chapters in this book explain the APEX system's approach to change management and include strategies to implement large-scale change.

The National Institute of Corrections continues to emphasize the importance of culture and change management in the correctional field. We hope that the APEX Initiative, with its Assessment Tools Protocol, Guidebook series, and Change Agent Training, assists agencies as they strive for excellence in organizational performance.

Morris Thigpen
Director
National Institute of Corrections

Preface

The National Institute of Corrections (NIC) and People in Charge are pleased to present the Achieving Performance Excellence (APEX) Guidebook series. The APEX Initiative began as NIC's Higher Performing Correctional Organization (HPCO) project in 2008. The HPCO project involved many correctional practitioners helping to identify the characteristics of a higher performing correctional organization. Practitioners and subject matter experts created a definition and a model of an HPCO based on the Baldrige Performance Excellence Program at the National Institute of Standards and Technology. The Baldrige Performance Excellence Program provides global leadership in the promotion and dissemination of standards of performance excellence. NIC is excited to bring this to correctional organizations around the country.

As HPCO progressed, it was renamed APEX and now includes three major developments: the APEX Assessment Tools Protocol, the APEX Public Safety Model and Guidebook series, and the APEX Change Agent Training.

The APEX Assessment Tools Protocol was developed during the years 2009–2011 to help correctional agencies identify their current organizational performance and areas to improve. Many correctional practitioners and agencies participated in the development, testing, and refinement of the tools in the protocol.

The APEX Guidebook evolved from one guidebook with information on the APEX model, its domains, and organizational change into a series of books. The Guidebook series is designed to provide resources, information, and processes to correctional organizations as they travel the path of organizational change leading to higher performance.

The APEX Change Agent Training will provide correctional agencies with capacity-building training and technical assistance in the APEX systems approach to organizational performance improvement.

Culture and Change Management: Using APEX To Facilitate Organizational Change is the third book in the series. It focuses on organizational culture and change management, offering practical suggestions for improving performance and creating positive change. These topics are critical for any organization that is seeking to maximize its potential for client, workforce, and operational success.

Respectfully submitted,

Nancy Cebula
People in Charge LLC
Owner and Principal Consultant

Theresa Lantz
People in Charge LLC
Criminal Justice Consultant

PEOPLE IN CHARGE

People in Charge is a small, woman-owned business that works with organizations and communities in the public and private sectors, helping them maximize their effectiveness through the participation of their people. Our focus is to help groups of people work together to build strong and vibrant organizations through participative planning, organizational design, and learning. You can learn more about People in Charge by visiting our website at *www.peopleincharge.org*.

Acknowledgments

The authors would like to acknowledge the following individuals for their contributions to this book:

Contributors

Pat Caruso, Director (Retired), Michigan Department of Corrections

Sherry Carroll, Correctional Program Specialist, National Institute of Corrections Administrative Division

Elizabeth Ritter, Writer and Editor, People in Charge

Abby Yannow, Leadership and Organizational Development Coach/Consultant

Reviewers

Margaret diZerega
Family Justice Program Director
Vera Institute of Justice

Kenny Massey
Undersheriff
Douglas County (KS) Correctional
Facility

And others at **People in Charge** who contributed:

Carlene Krogh
Editor
People in Charge

Lauren Piscopo
Writer and Editor
Greenest Living Writer

Pam McKinnie
Owner
Concepts Unlimited

Introduction to Achieving Performance Excellence

The APEX: Achieving Performance Excellence Initiative introduces a systems approach to change, specifically for correctional organizations, and incorporates multiple tools and strategies to assist agencies in building sustainable capacity for higher performance. The APEX Initiative includes the APEX Public Safety Model and its components, the APEX Assessment Tools Protocol, the APEX Guidebook series, and the APEX Change Agent Training. This initiative informs data-driven decisionmaking, enhances organizational change efforts, and provides support and resources to correctional agencies. At the heart of APEX is the fundamental mission of correctional organizations to maintain public safety, ensure safe and secure correctional supervision of offenders, and maintain safe and secure settings for those who work in the field. This comprehensive systems approach to continuous performance improvement encourages innovative ideas to enhance organizational operations, services, and processes and to achieve desired results.

APEX Guidebook Series Overview

The APEX Guidebook series presents a breadth and depth of information on the APEX Initiative, the APEX domains, and interventions and resources for correctional agencies to use as they implement organization improvement efforts. The series includes seven books, descriptions of which follow.

APEX: Building the Model and Beginning the Journey

This book gives a detailed description of the National Institute of Corrections' (NIC's) APEX Initiative, including the APEX Assessment Tools Protocol. The book presents reasons to self-assess and discusses change management and the benefits that correctional agencies can reap when they implement the APEX process.

Each of the APEX domains has a brief chapter devoted to defining it and the benefits of exploring the domain. "Overview to Achieving Performance Excellence" explains the various ways the APEX Initiative can be used in correctional agencies. "Developing a Communications Plan" describes in detail how agencies can inform stakeholders about their performance improvement journey, from the beginning through implementation and sustainability.

Culture and Change Management: Using the APEX Model To Facilitate Organizational Change

This book focuses in depth on organizational culture and change management in the correctional organization context, presenting a roadmap for correctional agencies to use as they begin a change initiative, whether it is a systemic change or a one-issue/intervention change.

Understanding Corrections through the APEX Lens

This book presents details on several of the APEX domains: Operations Focus (which includes Safe and Secure Supervision and Settings and Process Management); Stakeholder Focus; Strategic Planning; Workforce Focus; Measurement, Analysis, and Knowledge Management; and Results.

Achieving Performance Excellence: The Influence of Leadership on Organizational Performance

This book focuses on what individual leaders need to know and do as they develop their best leadership capabilities—the knowledge and practices necessary to lead people, organizations, and those outside the organization, including stakeholders, governing agencies, and the public, and gives the reader an opportunity to understand transactional and transformational leadership. Case studies from correctional agencies illustrate the concepts and provide realistic examples.

Applying the APEX Tools for Organizational Assessment

The APEX Assessment Tools Protocol includes three assessments that are corrections focused and user friendly. This self-assessment protocol includes the APEX Screener Tool (a short survey designed as a first step to assess readiness for change), the APEX Organizational Profile (a series of questions that help identify data, knowledge, and performance gaps in the organization), and the APEX Inventory (an indepth survey that rates performance in domains as well as readiness to change).

APEX Resources Directory Volumes 1 and 2

These volumes present numerous interventions and resources that agencies can use to help them build and implement their APEX change plans, deal with challenges and adjustments along the way, and sustain the changes. Volume 1 includes an introduction on how to use the NIC Information Center and sections on change management and each of the APEX domains and is designed to work with the reports from the APEX Assessment Tools. Volume 2 contains information on communication during times of change, focus groups, and team development; it also includes the NIC Information Center introduction.

USING THE ORGANIZATIONAL PROFILE

Fifteen staff and managers participated in the Organizational Profile to get a better idea of how their probation agency is dealing with its stakeholders and political environment. They learned that, although they are doing a pretty good job of dealing with their judicial overseers, there is a lack of trust and collaboration with other service providers in their jurisdiction. They downloaded several APEX books from the NIC website, including *Understanding Corrections through the APEX Lens* and the *APEX Resources Directory Volume 1*. They reviewed the sections on stakeholders to get ideas for increasing communication, building relationships, and improving collaborative initiatives with other agencies and external stakeholders as well as improving relationships with clients and their families.

The Guidebook series may be used in its entirety or in parts to suit the needs of agency personnel. The books in this series provide information, strategies, and tools to address the performance issues of correctional agencies. Use of the assessment tools is optional. Agency staff who know which topic they want to work on may go directly to the *APEX Resources Directory* or another book in the series for guidance.

How To Use APEX

The APEX Assessment Tools are designed for agencies to assess their organizational performance. The tools—Screener, Organizational Profile, and Inventory—were designed specifically for use in correctional agencies and are discussed in detail in *Applying the APEX Tools for Organizational Assessment.*

As an agency begins a change process, it can choose to use one or more of the APEX Assessment Tools, and it can cut and paste certain Guidebook chapters or strategies to target performance improvement areas. Because APEX is an agency-driven initiative, users can navigate the APEX materials and the tools to create a customized implementation plan. *APEX Resources Directory Volumes 1* and *2* provide access to other materials, tools, publications, and websites to tailor a specific performance improvement strategy.

Chapter 1: Introduction

Good cooks rely on principles, not recipes.

—Julia Child

The culture of an organization is one of the most influential factors in its ability to sustain a change effort. Deeper than the more superficial climate or morale, culture differs based on where it is on two continuums: between an external or internal focus, and between structure and control versus flexibility and agility. Chapter 2, "Organizational Culture and Change," focuses on this balance through the Competing Values Framework and discusses the four types of cultures that are created from the two continuums (see exhibit 1 in chapter 2 for an illustration of the framework).

Looking at where an organization falls on the Competing Values Framework helps point a path to successful change through the APEX (Achieving Public Excellence) Change Management Model. The groundwork for this model is laid out in chapter 3. Research on what enables successful change plans indicates that the human component is critical. Further research finds that engaging stakeholders through awareness, desire, knowledge, ability, and reinforcement is important for change to take place at all. Change efforts also succeed using Kotter's Eight-Step Process, detailed in this chapter.

The APEX Change Management Model is introduced in detail in chapter 4. Based on research and current best practices, it provides a step-by-step plan for creating and sustaining change that can be put to work in any correctional organization. A process map in this chapter helps illuminate how it all fits together to support change initiatives. Chapter 5 expands on this model, detailing elements for successful change that can become part of a successful plan.

Communication is central to any change effort, and chapter 6 explains how to put together a communications plan for change. This plan must be written with a focus on aligning with Prison Rape Elimination Act (PREA) standards, but should be adaptable to any communication issue. Chapter 7 includes an example of the APEX Change Management Process in action, presenting a case study where an agency shifted its culture to implement PREA standards. This detailed case study is complete with sample documents to enable others to follow this process. Chapter 8 contains an APEX Change Management Model with respect to reentry. Case studies of successful reentry change initiatives are cited and links to additional resources are provided.

Chapter 2: Organizational Culture and Change

If you want to change the culture, you will have to start by changing the organization.

—Mary Douglas

very organism, and every *organization* of organisms, must deal with two fundamental issues to survive within its environment. The need for balance is the same for individuals and all of their organizations, whether formal or informal, public or private, temporary or permanent.

First, an organization has to determine the value it will place on an internal focus to maintain its day-to-day processes as opposed to the value it will place on an external focus to monitor and respond to its environment. Second, an organization has to choose how much it will value stability and control to maintain its identity and structure as opposed to valuing flexibility and agility to adjust to changing demands. The choices an organization makes determine how well it will survive and thrive.

The concept of "culture" has a complicated history. In the past it referred to the cultivation of an appreciation of the arts or the pattern of human knowledge that depends on symbolic thought and social learning. The definition used most recently in examining organizational culture is: the shared assumptions, values, beliefs, attitudes, norms, and practices of an organization or group. The problem is that usually people do not have any clearer notion of exactly what "assumptions," "values," or "beliefs" are than they do of what is a "culture."

Instead of trying to define exactly what a culture is, it is easier to describe what a culture *does:* it tells people in an organization what will be expected of them and what they can expect of others. People will learn when they know what the expectations are, but more often they learn culture by watching others.

When people have been initiated into a shared organizational culture, they take for granted a set of assumptions, values, beliefs, and attitudes. Edgar Schein, a pioneer in the study of organizational culture, describes culture as "A pattern of shared basic assumptions that was learned by a group as it solved its problems of external adaptation and internal integration, that has worked well enough to be considered valid and, therefore, to be taught to new members as the correct way you perceive, think, and feel in relation to those problems" (Schein 2005:17).

Schein (1999) identifies three levels of organizational culture. The first level is what is seen in an organization—its formal structure and chain of command, position titles, policies, procedures, and public image. The second level is what an organization says, such as its mission and values statements, codes of conduct, and even the name it calls itself. The third level deals with tacit assumptions in the organization requiring indepth analysis.

The first two levels are easier to change than the third level. Organizations often do a paper implementation by making changes such as renaming a program, adopting a new mission and values statement, or rewriting policies or procedures. Mission and values statements are declarations of the *ideals* of an organization, not descriptions of the *realities* of daily behavior. An organization may have a value statement such as "We value open and honest

Note: "Organizational Culture and Change" was originally written by Christopher A. Innes, Ph.D.

communication throughout the agency" when the real value, as expressed in day-to-day behavior, may be closer to, "We value telling others only as much as we have to."

The majority of organizational change efforts fail because they are limited to the first two levels of organizational culture; they never reach beyond the ideals to confront the realities. Underlying these more visible layers is the third level: the deep assumptions that guide organizational culture and that can make or break any change effort. People immersed in a culture usually can only partly explain the unwritten rules or underlying assumptions. They just *know* what is right or wrong when they see it.

Many of the basic assumptions are erroneous or unflattering. For example, the belief that the organization is at the mercy of outside forces and has little control over its own future may produce a deep cynicism that is seldom voiced. The effect of reduced budgets and cutbacks by external forces may lead staff to believe they have no control over the future operations of the organization. Other cultural assumptions may concern human nature, such as if people can be trusted to do the right thing without being closely supervised, if they will always resist change, or if they usually act selfishly rather than for the common good of the organization. Finally, organizations develop their own rhythm based on their view of how quickly things should happen and if they believe a can-do attitude is more important than slower, more deliberative decisionmaking.

Because of their assumptions, organizational cultures often differ in the degree to which they want staff to respect authority or closely follow established procedures versus allowing staff more discretion and greater decisionmaking power. Compared to other industries, correctional agencies also experience uniquely traumatic experiences such as riots, homicides, staff misconduct, and high-profile crimes. An organization's history, combined with its culture, has a powerful effect on how the people within that organization perceive and respond to the challenges represented by external or internal pressures.

None of the differing assumptions, values, beliefs, or attitudes of a particular culture are necessarily wrong for that organization. Some thrive in a competitive culture based on self-interest while others survive in a culture based on a sense of duty and self-sacrifice. Which culture an organization adopts over time depends on the organization's purpose and whether its cultural framework helps achieve its goals. When a culture is no longer working,

CULTURE, CLIMATE, AND MORALE

How culture relates to climate and morale is often confusing, in part because research literature about climate or morale has not made the difference between them clear. Climate and morale are more superficial and change more easily than culture, often in response to temporary events such as a change in leadership. An organization needs to have a positive climate to do culture work, but a negative climate can be improved more easily than changing the culture. People in an organization may be unhappy or frustrated with how things are going at any one time, but that may not have anything to do with the fundamental beliefs and assumptions that underpin their organizational culture. Since dysfunctional cultures usually breed poor organizational climates, a first step in culture change is often to make symbolic gestures by fixing something particularly irritating or frustrating for staff (e.g., providing more dependable communication devices or increasing the use of video surveillance).

Source: D. Denison, "What is the Difference Between Organizational Culture and Organizational Climate?" *Academy of Management Review* 21:619–54, 1996.

however, organizations are faced with the complicated task of *deliberately* changing the cultural framework. If cultural frameworks are mostly unspoken and invisible, then directly changing them is difficult. Trying to argue people into changing their assumptions or values seldom works.

This gives rise to the truism, "You don't change cultures by trying to change cultures." Cultures are learned based on what works; therefore, to change a culture leaders have to show that something else works better. The success and sustainability of organizational change will ultimately rest on responses and adaptations to the challenges and changes in the environment that gave rise to the need for organizational change. Changing an organizational culture is like learning to ride a bicycle; one keeps trying until he/she stops falling off. When a change effort starts to encounter resistance, it is often because it chafes against the underlying cultural assumptions of the organization. Then the real work of cultural change actually begins. The Competing Values Framework, which has been used by correctional agencies across the country, is one approach for diagnosing and changing organizational cultures.

Competing Values Framework

The Competing Values Framework, based on the work of Kim Cameron and Robert Quinn (2006), suggests that every organization must balance competing values between an internal focus versus an external focus, and between structure and control versus flexibility and agility. Exhibit 1 illustrates this framework. The grid in the exhibit shows the four types of cultures that are created in their purest form, depending on where they are placed along the competing values dimensions.

An organization that places a higher value on the effective integration and a seamless unity of processes (internal focus) and also highly values reliability and clearly defined structures and roles (stability and control) is labeled *hierarchical* in this framework. This type of culture is very typically found in correctional organizations.

Exhibit 1: Competing Values Framework

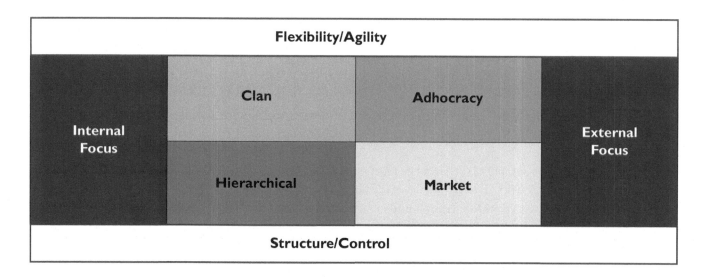

A very different type of culture exists when an organization places the same high value on effective integration and a seamless unity of processes (internal focus), but also highly values flexibility, discretion, and dynamic change (flexibility and agility). In the Competing Values Framework, this type of culture is labeled *clan* to capture the more familylike feel of organizations with this kind of culture. One way to contrast these two cultures is to say that in a hierarchical culture there is a strong emphasis on "doing things right," whereas in a clan culture the emphasis is on "doing things together." A common issue in correctional organizations is when there is the perception that the organization is too hierarchical and people want it to become more clanlike in the way it operates. Whenever there is a call for more teamwork or eliminating silos, it is a call for a more clanlike culture.

While hierarchical and clan cultures have an internal focus in common, two other cultural types (market and adhocracy) have an external focus; i.e., they place a high value on interacting with and/or competing against those outside the organization, such as customers, market competitors, and shareholders. These two cultures are more common in the private sector and differ from one another in the value they place on stability and control versus flexibility and agility.

An organization with an external focus that also highly values stability and control is labeled a *market* culture on the grid. By contrast, an organization with an external focus that also highly values flexibility and agility is labeled an *adhocracy*. This label is rooted in the phrase *ad hoc* and implies an organization that values a dynamic approach with specialized, often temporary, ways of organizing its work. While a market culture might emphasize "doing it fast," an adhocracy might emphasize "doing it first."

The type of culture an organization adopts as its primary framework depends on what works in achieving its goals. A company competing for business in an emerging high-tech field is more likely to prosper with an adhocracy culture and the leadership style and workforce development strategy that fit that type. The leadership style that works within an adhocracy is characterized by constant innovation and an entrepreneurial approach that stresses experimentation, risk taking, organizational agility, and continual reinvention. Such an organization would recruit, develop, and promote staff who thrive in an ever-changing workplace.

A correctional agency, on the other hand, would not last long if it adopted the same style. This does not mean that even the most hierarchical organization might not benefit from a little experimental risk taking. In fact, borrowing an element from a different cultural type and experimenting with it is a basic strategy for changing an organization's culture. For example, focusing on results enables an internally focused organization, such as a correctional agency, to move in an externally focused direction. Workforce development, on the other hand, could move the same organization toward a more clanlike culture. Many of the organizational change models proposed in recent years, such as Total Quality Management, reengineering, and downsizing, fit directly into the Competing Values Framework.

Keeping in mind that these are pure types used as examples, reviewing the details of each culture type helps to better understand how they work. Examining the leadership style, value orientation, theory of high performance and definition of success, and workforce development and preferred staff competencies gives one a sense about how it would feel to work within a particular culture. It also clarifies how disastrous it could be for an organization to have a leader with a style or a human resources strategy that clashes with its culture. The irony is, organizational change requires that a change must, to some degree, clash with the existing culture.

CULTURE TYPES

Adhocracy Culture

Description: Externally focused and valuing flexibility and decentralized decisionmaking intended to produce an organization that is agile, innovative, responsive, and constantly reinventing itself.

Value orientation: Creativity.

Theory of high performance: Innovation, expansive vision, and new resources will drive performance.

Definition of success: Leading the field in producing innovations.

Leadership type: Innovator, entrepreneurial, and visionary.

Human resources role: Fostering change and facilitating transformation.

Staff competencies: Systems thinking skills, organizational change abilities, collaborative, and consultative.

Market Culture

Description: Externally focused and valuing stability and control, this type of organization functions internally like a market by encouraging competition between units and rewarding bottom-line success.

Value orientation: Competition.

Theory of high performance: Competition and customer focus will drive performance.

Definition of success: Market share, achievement, profitability.

Leadership type: Hard driving, competitive, goal oriented, and productive.

Human resources role: Strategic business partner.

Staff competencies: Business and marketing skills, strategic analysis and leadership, achievement orientation.

Clan Culture

Description: Internally focused and valuing flexibility and decentralization, this type of organization values shared goals, participation, inclusiveness, and individuality.

Value orientation: Collaboration.

Theory of high performance: Individual development and participation will create higher performance.

Definition of success: Organizational commitment, participation, personal development, and familylike work environment.

Leadership type: Facilitator, mentor, and team builder.

Human resources role: Champion for employees, supportive, and responsive to employee needs.

Staff competencies: Good social and communication skills, cooperative, committed to organizational and personal development and improvement.

Hierarchical Culture

Description: Focused on rules, specialization, and accountability to produce an organization that functions smoothly and reliably.

Value orientation: Controlling.

Theory of high performance: Control and efficiency with well-defined and effective processes will produce higher performance.

Definition of success: Efficiency, timeliness, consistency, and stability.

Leadership type: Coordinator, monitor activity, and organizer.

Human resources role: Selection and assignment of specialists, skill maintenance and improvement, rule enforcement.

Staff competencies: Process orientation, customer relations, and service needs assessment.

These four types of organizational cultures provide a conceptual model that allows people to think through strategies to manage and change organizational cultures. No organization is a pure example of any one type, and most organizations mix different types depending on the roles and functions of the organization's different departments or divisions. In correctional facilities, line-level custody staff will have a different subculture from that of the central office. One of the strengths of the Competing Values Framework is an easy-to-use questionnaire, called the Organizational Culture Assessment Instrument (OCAI), which organizations can use to plot their location on the culture grid. This is incorporated into the APEX Inventory assessment tool. It can be found at *http://www.ocai-online.com/products/ocai-one*.

A Fresh Look at Correctional Cultures

Most correctional agencies, because of their public safety mission and militaristic, chain-of-command organizational structure, cluster in the hierarchical cultural type. The image of hierarchical cultures has usually been presented in negative terms in research, which is a reaction to what was perceived as the stifling cultures of rigid bureaucracies and the authoritarian leadership styles they employed. Rensis Likert (1961), for example, presented a typology of leadership styles that argued that the kinds of leadership and cultures typical of hierarchical organizations were to be avoided. In 1964, *The Managerial Grid* (Blake and Mouton 1964) labeled hierarchical cultures as having an "impoverished style" of management. While these theorists focused on corporate cultures, the tone they set toward hierarchical organizations has had a strong influence in how many view them, including those in corrections.

A better way of describing correctional culture from within the Competing Values Framework requires correctional organizations to look at the mission of corrections and how it has molded the organizational culture. Brad Bogue (2010) has pointed out that corrections shares a number of attributes with other high-reliability organizations that are characterized by complex, tightly interconnected processes intended to position the organization to respond instantly to potentially catastrophic events. Other examples of organizations that need to have high-reliability cultures are air traffic control, nuclear power plants, air and rail transportation systems, aircraft carrier deck operations, combat operations units in general, and firefighters. These seemingly very different types of organizations all share some essential elements that reveal the cultural characteristics they have in common.

Foremost among them is a *preoccupation with failure,* meaning that the organization strives to be constantly aware that any incident can mushroom into a crisis and that organizational readiness is essential (Weick and Sutcliffe 2001). This readiness involves close ongoing monitoring of operations to identify potential risks and respond to them quickly. In addition, a *reluctance to simplify* and *sensitivity to operations* are parts of the culture of a high-reliability organization. These organizations resist oversimplification of practices or processes by relying on redundancy, multiple levels of review, and close coordination across operational units to avoid gaps in the system. *Sensitivity to operations* refers to the close monitoring of operational details, frequent program reviews or audits, and preoccupation with adherence to operating procedures.

Two other characteristics of high-reliability organizations that are familiar to anyone working in correctional organizations are *deference to expertise* and a *commitment to resilience.* High-reliability organizations place a high value on expertise and skill, especially when they have been gained through years of hands-on experience. During critical incidents, agencies must have the capacity and the confidence in their staff to shift decisionmaking to the front lines where instant responses are necessary. A commitment to resilience is when organizations display a high level of organizational pride in meeting challenges and overcoming adversity. The camaraderie and morale commonly observed in high-reliability organizations such as correctional agencies is a fundamental expression of the cultural values underlying this type of organization. Like deference to expertise, commitment to resilience adds to the dynamic qualities of organizations and works to counterbalance the rigidity that a preoccupation with failure, reluctance to simplify, and sensitivity to operations can create in those same organizations.

From the perspective of the Competing Values Framework, high-reliability organizations can be seen as hierarchical organizations with values that are more clanlike. These values serve to keep the organization from becoming too rigid in its operational posture and allow it to pivot rapidly in a crisis. This mix of values has been learned by the organization and the profession at large as it has dealt with the unique challenges of working in corrections. This balance, however, can be upset when an organizational culture has "overlearned" these lessons; an organization may then be *too* preoccupied with failure to the point that it avoids any risks, relies too heavily on command and control, and is inflexible in its operations.

The idea of cultural change may actually be a misnomer—what most correctional agencies need to do is to rebalance their culture by bringing forward and emphasizing expertise and resilience.

Discussing cultural issues in a correctional setting from the rebalancing perspective may be a more constructive approach. Rather than stressing the need for cultural change, the message from leadership can be to focus on the need to rebalance or restore the culture. The goal is then to bring back the core values of *expertise* and *resilience* in the face of challenges. Framed in this way, many of the problems associated with the idea of forcing people to change are avoided.

Since 2000, the National Institute of Corrections (NIC) has been carrying out a project on prison culture that seeks to help institutions assess and change their cultures. Dozens of institutions were assessed by a team of outside correctional professionals during a multiday, onsite visit. The assessment used a number of techniques, including observation of operations on all shifts, individual interviews and discussions with focus groups comprising staff and incarcerated individuals, and the administration of a modified version of Cameron and Quinn's (2006) OCAI. NIC found that the current culture was skewed heavily toward the lower left corner of the grid (the hierarchical culture), while the preferred culture tended much more toward the upper left corner of the grid (the clan culture). Issues raised by staff in interviews and focus groups involved problems with communication, mutual respect, lack of trust, and similar themes that point to a desire for a more clanlike organizational culture.

Institutions assessed in this project participated because they had intractable problems that they identified as being cultural, at least in part. The dissatisfaction of the staff may be due to the lack of deference to expertise and a commitment to resilience. This does not mean the staff had a theory of how a high-reliability organization should operate, but it could mean that they had an intuition that their organization was not working the way it should. Their frustration does not mean that they want to replace their culture with a clan culture, but they do want to see their culture become more balanced.

Leadership and Culture Change

In a typical hierarchical correctional organization, cultural rebalancing nearly always requires a special brand of leadership, and transformational leaders are the most effective in creating changes within an organization (Eggers and Gray 2012). The concept of transformational leadership is part of the Full Range Leadership Model (Bass and Avolio 1994). This model compares three types of leadership: laissez-faire, transactional, and transformational. In contrast to the first two, transformational leaders are able to motivate staff to go beyond where they would otherwise be willing to go.

THREE TYPES OF LEADERSHIP

Transactional: Based on exchanges between leaders/followers.

Laissez-faire: Lack of leadership, "anything goes" sense of responsibility.

Transformational: Encourages change, makes it possible for others to take responsibility and be accountable.

"The transactional leader works within the organizational culture as it exists; the transformational leader changes the organizational culture" (Bass and Avolio 1994:24). Transformational leaders influence staff by increasing awareness of the importance of achieving organizational goals, creating a vision and required implementation strategy, motivating staff commitment to the organization, and encouraging personal development and organizational excellence. A transformational leader is one who influences staff by acting as a role model, creating inspiration, encouraging innovative thinking, and functioning as a coach or mentor to individual staff (Bass and Avolio 1994). In the Competing Values Framework, a transformational leadership style is characteristic of an adhocracy or clan culture. If a hierarchical culture such as corrections adopts this style, it should move the organization into a more balanced, high-reliability organization.

Positive leadership (Cameron 2008) is another management style that transforms organizations. In this style, extraordinary performance is *expected* in the organization. "Without being Pollyannaish, it emphasizes positive communication, optimism, and strength as well as the values and opportunity embedded in problems and weaknesses" (Cameron 2008:2). Positive organizations focus on thriving by stressing the strengths, capacities, and potential of staff as well as by creating an organization that works to facilitate the best of the human condition and foster organizational virtuousness.

ORGANIZATIONAL VIRTUOUSNESS

Virtuous organizations are those that provide a positive environment for workers, clients, and stakeholders. They have organizational goals that are meaningful, as well as policies and practices that provide benefit to their customers/clients, workforce, and other stakeholders. There are three characteristics that help define the virtuous organization: human impact, moral goodness, and social betterment:

- **Human impact.** The organization hires people with moral character and meaningful purpose and creates an environment where coworkers treat each other and stakeholders fairly.

- **Moral goodness.** The organization is value driven and its goals, policies, and procedures reflect what is good and right.

- **Social betterment.** The organization's results produce benefit to others.

Source: K. Cameron, J. Dutton, and R. Quinn, *Positive Organizational Scholarship: Foundations of a New Discipline* (San Francisco: Berrett-Kohler, 2003).

Correctional leaders struggling with a dysfunctional culture may see a leadership change as an unrealistic goal, but the concepts of transformational and positive leadership styles are well grounded in research and practice (Cameron 2008). The styles can be broken down into specific strategies and actions that correctional administrators, managers, and line supervisors can learn and use. Cameron (2008), for example, lists four organizational development strategies that create a more positive and higher performing organizational culture:

1. Creating a positive tone in the organizational climate.

2. Promoting positive interpersonal relationships with and between staff.

3. Stressing positive communication at all levels of the organization.

4. Infusing purpose and meaning into the work life of all staff.

There is no shortage of culture change resources, including theories, books, training programs, and consultants, each with their own set of principles, concepts, strategies, and techniques. Most have been tried in organizations, including corrections, and most have failed to produce lasting change, mainly because change is not a theoretical exercise. Cultures are learned in the first place and are maintained because they seem to work; new cultures will be learned and maintained only if they work better than the old culture.

A useful way to think about what an organization needs to do is to look at what it is trying to accomplish: (1) fix a specific problem, (2) work to improve how things are done, or (3) implement something new. When working to improve how things are done, the goal is to increase the efficiency or effectiveness of existing operations, practices, or processes. Improvements are not fundamental changes to operations—they only make the current way of doing things work better. On the other hand, when an organization is trying to innovate, it is seeking a new, more effective way of doing things. The difference is that a successful innovation will achieve higher levels of performance than the old way of doing things, *even when the old way was working as well as it could.* Since innovation is much more costly and difficult than a simpler improvement, an organization must very carefully consider whether an investment in a large-scale innovation effort is feasible and will be worth it.

Deciding which of these two—organizational development versus organizational innovation—will be attempted is fundamentally strategic. Boonstra (2004) draws a distinction between *planned change* and the kind of organizational development referred to here as organizational *innovation.* Planned change is more limited in scope and focuses on incremental improvements in the existing organization and its culture. For example, Cameron (2008) lists *positive communication* as one of the most effective ways to improve organizational performance. Research has shown that just increasing the ratio of positive messages to negative ones has a measurable effect on performance. Positive statements include expressions of appreciation, support, helpfulness, approval, and compliments, whereas negative statements express criticism, disapproval, dissatisfaction, cynicism, or disparagement. Greater use of more positive statements and fewer negative ones has a powerful effect on an organization's climate and culture.

Before an organization undertakes the intensive work of a lengthy cultural change process, it needs to know if it is really ready. Many of the organizations involved in the NIC culture project had dysfunctional cultures, but were not ready to change because the organization as a whole was not working. These organizations did not consistently follow the accepted standards of professional practice in corrections, and the assessment team was able to point to clear deficiencies. Other organizations worked well enough, but the more objective observers on the team identified areas of correctional policy or practice that could be improved. An organization with basic deficiencies or where simpler operational improvements are available is unwise to try large-scale efforts for change. However, if an organization is ready to undertake such a transformation, correctly implementing the change is crucial to long-term success.

Implementation of Culture Change

Implementation has now become an evidence-based practice. A clear, step-by-step process can be used to make permanent changes to an organization. Dean Fixsen and his colleagues (2005) at the National Implementation Research Network have led the way in synthesizing this body of knowledge. They define implementation as the art and science of incorporating into the routine practice of an organization an innovative policy, practice, or program. "According to this definition, implementation processes are purposeful and are described in sufficient detail such that an independent observer can detect the presence and strength of the 'specific set of activities' related to implementation" (Fixsen et al. 2005:5). Implementation is not about what people see or what an organization says, it is about what an organization does. Paper or process implementations focus on the surface aspects of the culture, but real implementation has to be about the underlying behavior of the organization. To implement anything, specific people within an organization must perform specific activities that are visible, verifiable, and represent new patterns of doing the work. Successful implementation occurs when a well-planned and purposeful program is executed through each stage of the process.

IMPLEMENTATION FIDELITY

■ The degree to which an innovative program follows the original program design.

■ The faithful implementation of the program's components.

Source: S. Mihalic, K. Irwin, A. Fagan, D. Ballard, and D. Elliott, *Successful Program Implementation: Lessons From Blueprints* (Washington, DC: U.S. Department of Justice, Office of Justice Programs, Office of Juvenile Justice and Delinquency Prevention, 2004).

The first step in the Fixsen et al. (2005) model is *exploration and sustainability*. Failing to invest the resources and take the time necessary to complete this step causes most implementation failures. During this step, the leadership, the Change Team, and a staff workgroup or advisory committee must identify precisely what the change being proposed will involve, what evidence shows that it is a workable solution for the organization, whether it is feasible to adopt the change, and how the organization can be prepared for the change. This group also has to assess whether resources are available to implement and sustain the change, how fidelity in the implementation will be monitored and maintained, how success will be measured, and how turnover will be managed to renew the effort as personnel change.

Cameron and Quinn (2006) have a six-step process for change that essentially expands on the first step of the Fixsen et al. (2005) model. The first two steps in their process involve the development of agreement by key staff, including those who will be directly involved in the culture change effort, on what the current culture is and what the desired future culture should look like. It is important that this process be inclusive and that it involve all of the important subgroups within the organization who are essential to success. The next stage is a review to determine what the change from the current to the desired future culture will and will not mean for the organization and each of its subgroups. Cameron and Quinn (2006) label the fourth step in the process "identify illustrative stories" to point to the need for an organization to create a shared narrative of the history and future of the organization. They say "… the team should identify two or three incidents or events that illustrate the key values they want to permeate the future organizational culture" (Cameron and Quinn 2006:97). These are success stories that can be used as examples of the organization at its best, especially stories that highlight expertise and resilience. The fifth and sixth steps are to develop a strategic plan and an implementation plan. In the Fixsen et al. (2005) model, the implementation plan is expanded into five more steps.

After the initial groundwork has been done, the next step in the Fixsen et al. (2005) model is to launch the installation stage of the change initiative. During installation, all of the necessary people and resources are put into place. If staff need to be hired, reassigned, relocated, trained, equipped, or supplied, this should be done, together with all of the necessary bureaucratic adjustments to infrastructure, rules, and regulations. The installation stage is the next opportunity to familiarize the organization with the change.

The third stage, initial implementation, is where many organizations begin and soon fail. It is usually the first time that the people working in the organization really see changes taking place, and often they do not like what they see. Change in theory is too abstract to arouse much concern, particularly in organizations where change efforts have come and gone many times before. Change is probably not real unless it is uncomfortable; it is at the point of initial implementation that behaviors are changing and the underlying assumptions of the organization's culture are being challenged. A higher degree of tension, raised voices, and some melodrama can be expected, which should be welcomed rather than suppressed or ignored. Ignoring difficult issues is part of what has maintained the undesirable culture in the first place.

Moving from initial implementation to full implementation is an incremental process as the innovation expands across and is integrated into the practices and procedures of the organization as a whole. The tasks of full implementation include maintaining and improving skills and activities, integration and coordination, and changes in policy to adjust to new ways of operating. Most initial implementations take place in pilot sites that have been chosen because they are a more friendly organizational territory, so full implementation usually involves expanding into less hospitable parts of the organization. Hopefully, the organization learned enough lessons during the initial implementation to be equipped to anticipate and respond to most of the issues that arise during the full implementation.

Each attempted implementation of an innovation will also create opportunities for more improvement as it becomes an accepted part of the way things are done in that organization. The *innovation* stage begins to emerge from the process of full implementation when staff stop coping with the change and start making further improvements. Unfortunately, some of the suggested "improvements" may simply be backsliding or may represent a drift away from the original goals of the change effort. The best way to avoid either backsliding or drift is to ensure that the innovation has been fully implemented with fidelity before beginning any modifications.

Finally, a distinct stage of sustainability needs to take place, during which the effects of the change settle into the organization's culture. The challenge during this stage is to renew the change as turnover brings new staff into the organization as other staff leave.

Immunity to Change

Any change, even a change for the better, is always accompanied by drawbacks and discomforts.

—*Arnold Bennett*

In the brief presentations above on leadership types, change, and implementation, the many difficulties of making changes in an organization and its culture have been noted only in passing. The actual implementation of a large-scale change in any organization rarely proceeds smoothly through a set of predictable stages.

Robert Kegan and Lisa Lahey (2009) have closely examined the idea of "immunity to change" as a predictable and manageable transition point in any change process. Kegan and Lahey provide a structured approach to developing an immunity map that has proved useful for guiding change efforts in a number of settings. Mapping out the process of undertaking change first involves developing a clearly defined improvement goal. This is what should have come out of the exploration and sustainability stage of the implementation process. The second step requires a fearless inventory of what the organization is doing (or not doing) that works against accomplishing the goal; how the organization has defined its current and preferred future culture should have shed light on how it works against itself.

The difficult work of describing what people do to reinforce the current culture and create obstacles to the preferred culture should be done thoroughly. An honest examination of how the existing culture is perpetuated provides insights into the unacknowledged values, assumptions, and beliefs that constitute that culture. Holman

(2010) has used the concept of "engaging emergence" to explore a number of practical approaches to help an organization both uncover its assumptions and envision itself in alternative ways. One of the best ways to reveal the role of cultural assumption is to do the opposite of the usual practices.

At the individual level, this occurs when people begin the action stage of change, whereas at the organizational level it starts at the initial implementation stage. What is labeled as denial or resistance and treated as an obstacle to progress can just as easily be seen as a natural reaction to changing conditions.

Summary

The paradox of changing organizational cultures is that they do not change by *trying* to change. They change by changing *behavior,* and behavior changes when the new way of doing things works better than the old way. Resistance to change, even sharp conflict within the organization, is part of the process—the growing pains that accompany any significant change. During the installation and initial implementation stages, there are many opportunities to encounter and work through these issues. Taking the time and energy to do so will provide the organization with the essential knowledge to proceed to full implementation and sustainability.

Using the Competing Values Framework helps an organization see how to proceed in the quest for higher performance. It provides a valuable framework for understanding the organization's culture and how that culture supports or hinders the organization's growth. The next chapters offer guidance and examples to consider when putting these concepts into practice.

References

Bass, B., and B. Avolio. 1994. *Improving Organizational Effectiveness through Transformational Leadership.* Thousand Oaks, CA: Sage Publications.

Blake, R., and J. Mouton. 1964. *The Managerial Grid: The Key to Leadership Excellence.* Houston: Gulf Publishing Company.

Bogue, B. 2010. "How Principles of High Reliability Organizations Relate to Corrections." *Federal Probation* 73:22–27.

Boonstra, J. 2004. "Dynamics of Organization Change and Learning: Reflections and Perspectives." In J. Boonstra (ed.), *Dynamics of Organizational Change and Learning.* Chichester, West Sussex, England: Wiley Books.

Cameron, K., J. Dutton, and R. Quinn. 2003. *Positive Organizational Scholarship: Foundations of a New Discipline.* San Francisco: Berrett-Kohler.

Cameron, K., and R. Quinn. 2006. *Diagnosing and Changing Organizational Culture.* San Francisco: Jossey-Bass.

Cameron, K. 2008. *Positive Leadership: Strategies for Extraordinary Performance.* San Francisco: Berrett-Koehler.

Denison, D. 1996. "What is the Difference Between Organizational Culture and Organizational Climate?" *Academy of Management Review* 21:619–54.

Eggers, J., and J. Gray. 2012. "Leadership That is Transforming." In N. Cebula, E. Craig, J. Eggers, M. Douville Fajardo, J. Gray, and T. Lantz (eds.), *Achieving Performance Excellence: The Influence of Leadership on Organizational Performance.* Washington, DC: U.S. Department of Justice, National Institute of Corrections.

Fixsen, D., S. Naoom, K. Blase, R. Friedman, and F. Wallace. 2005. *Implementation Research: A Synthesis of the Literature.* Tampa, FL: National Implementation Research Network.

Holman, P. 2010. *Engaging Emergence.* San Francisco: Berrett-Koehler.

Kegan, R., and L. Lahey. 2009. *Immunity to Change.* Boston: Harvard Business Press.

Likert, R. 1961. *New Patterns of Management.* New York: McGraw-Hill.

Mihalic, S., K. Irwin, A. Fagan, D. Ballard, and D. Elliott. 2004. *Successful Program Implementation: Lessons From Blueprints.* Washington, DC: U.S. Department of Justice, Office of Justice Programs, Office of Juvenile Justice and Delinquency Prevention.

Schein, E. 1999. *The Corporate Culture Survival Guide.* San Francisco: Jossey-Bass.

Schein, E.H. 2005. *Organizational Culture and Leadership,* 3d ed. San Francisco: Jossey-Bass.

Weick, K., and K. Sutcliffe. 2001. *Managing the Unexpected: Assuring High Performance in an Age of Complexity.* San Francisco: Jossey-Bass.

Chapter 3: Introduction to Change Management

This chapter presents information on managing change and the results to be expected, and offers development and implementation guidelines for correctional organizations engaged in large-scale cultural change. It lays the groundwork for the next chapter on the APEX Change Management Model.

Barrier Points to Change Management

The most successful change management strategies take the human side of change management into account. Studies of 1,500 organizations where 90 percent of change management failed took human motivation for granted. In correctional organizations, virtually everything involves human factors; every new procedure involves changing human behavior to at least some degree. If new standard operating procedures are not implemented or Prison Rape Elimination Act (PREA) action requirements are ignored, poor change management execution is the first place to look for the root cause of failure. Whether transforming entire systems or executing one-time interventions, change management is a key performance determinant.

The five best change management practices have been identified and validated through research by Prosci, a non-profit organization specializing in the study of successful change efforts. When Prosci founder Jeff Hiatt studied Bell Labs engineering project failures, he discovered that most breakdowns occurred when all of the project management milestones indicated they should *not* have broken down. Looking into the causes (using many of the project analysis and process improvement tools available in the *APEX Resources Directory Volume 1*), Hiatt discovered that 90 percent of project management failures occurred because of failure to recognize what he calls the "people side of change."

After testing, questioning, and conducting postmortems on these failed projects, Hiatt identified five barrier points that are arranged in a hierarchy and that if not fully addressed in order, will exponentially increase the chance of project failure. These rules for shaping human behavior to be able to create and sustain change apply universally; the results coincide with the APEX best practice case results (Hiatt 2006).

Change management is unlikely to be successful without establishing the following:

- **Awareness.** Everyone who is expected to implement or support the change must be aware of what is happening and why, what the intended result is, and what role each individual is expected to play in creating the difference between the current state and the future state.

- **Desire.** Everyone who in any way can influence the outcome of the change effort must have the desire to help make it happen. They must know what is in store for them if the change is successful and, conversely, if the effort should fail. Desire cannot happen without first creating and firmly anchoring awareness. A complete change management strategy will entail mapping out the entire organization of management team members,

Note: "Introduction to Change Management" was originally written by Tanya Rhone.

staff, stakeholders, and anyone else who needs to support the effort. Those directing the change effort will need to assess each member of the organization to determine who is and is not on board, how to best convince those who are resistant, and how to develop a contingency plan to deal with their lack of support if it cannot be obtained. Many a project, change effort, culture change initiative, and simple process alteration has been derailed by an influential negative person. If the project is worth doing, this is worth addressing.

- **Knowledge.** Those called on to implement the change must know not only what is expected, but they must also have the knowledge to carry it out. Change efforts often begin with a facsimile of this element in the form of a directive, memorandum, staff rollcall announcement, bulletin, or other type of proclamation. If the change fails, it is often the case that those called on to carry out the order are not aware of what it really means to them and the organization. If the first two barrier points are met, knowledge can and should be next. It is the third barrier point that will block perfect execution.

- **Ability.** Knowing *how* is the essential outcome of knowledge. Having the ability to carry out the change process may involve personal training, instruction, on-the-job practice, mentorship, and/or coaching. Watching a training video alone does not create competitive, world-class ability. People can be aware of what is required and their personal role in the change, become fully engaged with the desire to do their part, and know what is expected and how to do their jobs; however, if they lack the ability, resources, or infrastructure to carry out the required change, the effort will likely fail.

- **Reinforcement.** After the change effort begins, it needs continuous reinforcement. This comes in face-to-face conversations between employees and their supervisors, from the senior official, and from those in the most influential positions to make the message understood and real. Reinforcement is not a one-time requirement. It must be done at least seven times and through different channels and media. Failure to reinforce a change initiative is a barrier point that can kill the effort.

Prosci (Hiatt 2006) calls this the ADKAR model (Awareness, Desire, Knowledge, Ability, and Reinforcement). Whether the change is a simple project management initiative or a complex culture change transformation, failure to execute at any of these ADKAR barrier points will kill most change efforts. This applies to all projects that require people to change what they are doing now and begin doing something different. As the previous chapter demonstrates, people naturally resist change. Most change efforts in correctional organizations do not require transformational change. Changing a standard operating procedure for intake or classification is not normally expected to disrupt the lives of staff too much or encounter too many roadblocks, or even passive resistance. Even in these cases, however, the five barrier points still apply (Hiatt 2006).

Kotter's Eight Steps

Corrections best practices in change management that result in large-scale organizational culture change all appear to take the five barrier points into account. In addition to the barrier points, these more complex change initiatives include eight qualities or attributes. To varying degrees, and sometimes in a different order, all successful culture change initiatives resemble an approach to successful organizational change suggested by Dr. John P. Kotter, a Harvard Business School professor and organizational change management authority (Kotter 1996).

Kotter's eight-step process (Kotter 1996; Kotter and Rathgeber 2006) for successful change efforts is as follows:

1. **Increase urgency.** Behavior precedes attitudes. By creating a sense of urgency among influential stakeholders, people can become "pumped up" and inspired to want to change. The sense of urgency gets people ready to take action.

2. **Build the change team.** A Change Team is made up of people from each level within the agency who have the skills and desire to make the effort succeed. Members should be the kinds of people who are credible, have good reputations, and act as an extension of senior management.

3. **Get the vision right.** Establish a simple vision that focuses on emotional triggers that explain what is changing and what the new desired state will look like, who will be involved, and what will change. This vision should also explain what will not be altered, clearly defining the boundaries to exclude any unacceptably dangerous strategies and setting the stage for making the vision a reality in the most effective way. This vision message can be articulated in a "1-minute elevator speech" or in two short sentences. Make the statement emotionally powerful enough to touch stakeholders' heartstrings.

> Martin Luther King did not say, *"I have a change management plan."* He proclaimed, *"I have a dream."*

4. **Communicate for buy-in.** Engage as many people as possible. Communicate the essentials simply in a way that appeals and responds to people's needs. Do the homework to understand what people are feeling and address their needs with simple, heartfelt messages. Use different channels that declutter communications and leverage technology. The goal is to create awareness and a desire to change at the gut level. Symbols speak loudly in this type of communication and repetition is important.

5. **Empower action.** Remove obstacles, enable constructive feedback, and build opportunities for senior management to provide support. Provide the training, knowledge, and skills employees need to make change happen because without the ability to do what is expected, it will be impossible for employees to make the desired change. Commitment will increase in relation to the opportunity to contribute.

6. **Create short-term wins.** Set easy-to-achieve, bite-sized goals and a manageable number of initiatives, being careful to complete current stages before starting new ones. Encourage broad participation that assigns responsibility for outcomes and holds individuals personally accountable for results.

7. **Do not let up.** Encourage ongoing progress reporting on achieved and future milestones that focus on tangible performance gains and concrete proof of effectiveness.

8. **Make change stick.** Continuous reinforcement from both supervisors and senior executives is critical to sustaining any change effort. Tolerating low commitment to change is an invitation to mediocrity that inhibits the process of weaving the desired change into the culture. Continuous reinforcement through frequent communication with staff is an effective way to make the change stick.

Much of the good, qualitative information used to inform a strong change management strategy comes from understanding stakeholder positions. One desired outcome of the stakeholder analysis is to understand the problem landscape of change resistance. John Kotter (1996) offers this guidance for engaging stakeholders:

1. **See.** They must visualize the problems and successes during the change process. Dramatic, compelling situations must be experienced, captured, and shared.

2. **Feel.** When people see something new that is compelling to them, they have a visceral response that reduces negative emotions, complacency, and cynicism.

3. **Change.** Emotionally charged ideas change behavior and reinforce that change.

HERE'S WHAT'S IN IT FOR YOU

When holding initial discussions with stakeholders, it is important to acknowledge all of their ideas. The trap to avoid is creating the impression that all wishes can come to pass. Instead, internal and external stakeholder interactions are aimed at engaging interested parties in a variety of ways with custom-designed messages to prepare the ground for the change effort. The object is to convey the change messages and collect information to build support. The message is: "Here's what's in it for you."

Considering both the Kotter literature (Kotter 1996; Kotter and Cohen 2002; Kotter and Rathgeber 2006) and the Prosci ADKAR model (Hiatt 2006) in light of the corrections best practices that were studied to develop the APEX Guidebook series, a correctional model for large-scale organizational change begins to emerge. This model can guide cultural transformation, resulting in an organizational climate capable of yielding higher performance and limited only by the resources and resourcefulness of the senior management team.

Summary

Organizations that want to change but do not take the human side of change management into account are statistically more likely to fail than those that invest in the human side of the organization. Prosci (Hiatt 2006) identifies five key factors that management needs to focus on when considering the human component: awareness, desire, knowledge, ability, and reinforcement. Failure to consider these factors constitutes a barrier to success. Kotter's (1996) eight-step process includes the following qualities or attributes of successful organizational change: creating urgency, building a Change Team, getting the vision right, communicating for buy-in, empowering action, creating short-term wins, not letting up, and making change stick. The next chapter introduces the APEX Change Management Model.

References

Hiatt, J.M. 2006. *ADKAR: A Model for Change in Business, Government and Our Community.* Loveland, CO: Prosci.

Kotter, J. 1996. *Leading Change.* Boston: Harvard Business School Press.

Kotter, J.P., and D.S. Cohen. 2002. *The Heart of Change.* Boston: Harvard Business School Press.

Kotter, J., and H. Rathgeber. 2006. *Our Iceberg Is Melting.* New York: St. Martin's Press.

Chapter 4: APEX Change Management Model

The APEX Change Management Model (see exhibit 2) is a systems approach to changing organizations. It works as a roadmap for navigating organizational change efforts leading to the high-performance organizational culture introduced earlier in this book. It is based on the current literature and best practices for organizational behavior change, especially the most successful practices found in correctional operating environments for implementing new policies and practices that improve performance and large-scale cultural change. What follows in this chapter is a systemwide approach to change, recognizing that each part of the organization is affected in the short term and long term by intervention efforts. This chapter will examine this change management process and its applicability to the field of corrections.

Exhibit 2: APEX Change Management Model

Stage 1 — Plan and Assess

Stage 2 — Define the Goal

Stage 3 — Organize for Results

Stage 4 — Plan the Implementation Strategy

Stage 5 — Implement the Change Management Plan

Stage 6 — Sustain the Change Effort

Changing a correctional culture can be an enormous undertaking. The magnitude of disruption caused by alterations in work relationships, mindset shifts, stakeholder involvement in operations, exposure to risk, potential productivity increase, distraction from routine duties, or plain hard work usually exceeds anything else that can be planned. The APEX Change Management Model reduces the risk of large-scale culture change project management failure and increases both the speed of change transition and the agency's ability to sustain the effort over the long term.

Stage 1: Plan and Assess

Thorough preparation and planning consider the organization's operating environment, the conditions requiring change, and the agency's readiness to accept change. This work leads to more efficient, complete, and faster change implementation and increases the chance for long-term sustainability. Correctional agencies assess their current organizational performance using quantitative and qualitative data-gathering methods; using both methods will give a more comprehensive picture than if either one is used alone. Both are valid sources of information and require time for data gathering and analysis. Qualitative data such as focus group results and employee surveys are descriptive and lead to more nuanced interpretations. Quantitative data such as the APEX Screener are definitive, numeric, and open to statistical analysis. In stage 1, all of these data are separated into two distinct parts: informal assessment or screening, and readiness determination.

Informal Assessment

Something always causes a correctional agency to think about changing. The stimulus may be as basic as a policy update to incorporate new requirements, a practice that should begin or stop, or a process that has grown inefficient over the years. Stronger incentives to consider change might derive from the way the agency is organized to achieve its mission, a reorganization mandated by legislation, a problem affecting a broader community of interests, or a difficult set of circumstances drawing attention from outside the agency (e.g., the requirements of a legal settlement). Perhaps the decision to consider change is both new and internal, as in the appointment of a new director or chief, or a requirement to conform to an evidence-based practice that leads to the conclusion that the easiest way to adopt it is to change something. Change efforts can also come about as a result of going through an assessment, audit, or accreditation process. Whatever triggers a discussion about change, the wise thing to do first is to assess the agency in a variety of areas. The APEX Public Safety Model (see exhibit 3), with its eight domains, and the APEX Assessment Tools Protocol offer correctional agencies an ideal set of tools for this analysis.

Agency Self-Assessment

Agencies have many channels in which to complete self-assessments. These include such familiar processes and studies as:

- Policy reviews.

- Work process reviews.

- Security audits.

- Staff or stakeholder surveys.

- The APEX Screener, Organizational Profile, and Inventory.

- Other assessment instruments.

These assessments focus on one or more areas needing resolution or improvement. They are often effective for what they are intended to accomplish; however, no single review, survey, or audit is designed to cover all of the

Exhibit 3: APEX Public Safety Model

Note: The vertical, two-headed arrow pointing from the measurement, analysis, and knowledge management domain to the rest of the domains illustrates its foundational nature. The other two-headed arrows indicate the importance of feedback—a critical component of a higher performing correctional agency.

domains useful to corrections (except for the APEX Assessment Tools Protocol). The objective of assessment is to find and analyze all of the quantitative and qualitative data available to make informed decisions on the feasibility of successful change and how to approach it.

Assessing Readiness To Change

Nobody likes change like a wet baby.

—Mark Twain

Assessing readiness to change is one of the most essential tasks to complete when change is first contemplated. Data-driven decisions and evidence-based practices should shape a well-executed preparatory planning phase to gauge the feasibility of going forward with the change effort. In some cases, the status quo is a better position than a failed culture change initiative that is laden with ill will among staff, stakeholders, and the leadership team. Ultimately the planning effort leads to a go or no-go decision, in which "go" indicates a high probability of success and "no go" signals that the risks outweigh the likelihood of success.

Assessing readiness becomes more critical when the main driver of change is public or political pressure to "do something." This can build a sense of urgency, but it should not be at the expense of readiness preparation and planning. In one case, public outcry grew so loud and influential that silencing the media became the action driver, leaving little time or patience to develop readiness for any changes.

Examining Current Policies and Operating Practices

Scrutinizing current policies and operating practices provides data that will reveal the current organizational landscape. The end result may be a list of problems, opportunities, concerns, and consequences that offer data on current policies and practices. Consider all of the policies and practices that drive and restrain the change effort, such as:

■ What guidance documents affect or are affected by this initiative?

■ What might the proposed change effort impact?

■ What policy issues could drive the necessity for change?

■ What policy issues could potentially discourage change?

■ What operating practices have caused the agency to undertake the change effort?

■ What operating practices represent major roadblocks to success or require careful risk assessment?

Reviewing Outside Information Sources

The National Institute of Corrections (NIC) offers a host of free and easily accessed off-the-shelf information resources and agency knowledge of correctional practices, as well as some histories of the results of change initiatives in different jurisdictions. It is important to document everything that is reviewed and the lessons provided by each case analysis. Organizing this material in some way, such as in a table, saves reviewers and other team members the painstaking task of rereading each best practice summary.

Other resources to check include think tank research from the Bureau of Justice Statistics, Pew Charitable Trusts, Pew Research Center, Urban Institute, Vera Institute of Justice, Council of State Governments, and other organizations that offer relevant information, reports, and data at no cost that are accessible online. Professional organizations, including the American Probation and Parole Association, American Jail Association, Association of State Correctional Administrators (ASCA), and American Correctional Association also provide applicable information.

APEX Assessment Tools Protocol

The APEX Assessment Tools Protocol includes the APEX Screener, the APEX Organization Profile, and the APEX Inventory. These self-assessment tools are based on the APEX Public Safety Model and the Baldrige Performance Excellence Program; they provide correctional agencies with a durable framework for guiding, planning, and assessing their performance and results in challenging and rapidly changing times. The agency is solely in control of how the data are used or shared, with no expectation that they will be shared with NIC or any other entity.

■ **The APEX Screener** is a brief, self-administered survey that looks at organizational readiness for change. This Excel-based survey can be filled out by agency management and staff. It includes 24 items that help focus discussion on organizational preparedness, readiness for change, and performance in the APEX Public Safety Model domains.

- **The APEX Organizational Profile** looks at the organization's operations, environment, relationships, and situation. This series of questions provides a vehicle for review, analysis, and targeted discussion. As the agency's leaders and staff respond to the questions, they learn about the organization and identify gaps in data, knowledge, and performance measures.

- **The APEX Inventory** is a more comprehensive assessment of the eight APEX domains and evaluates the organization's readiness for change more thoroughly than the APEX Screener. The questions are designed to let the executive team have focused discussions on how the agency is performing in the eight APEX domains and how ready it is to begin a change process. The questions also provide enough information to enable the agency to create a systemic performance improvement implementation plan.

These tools provide a comprehensive, systems-based picture of how the organization operates in the eight domains, and they inform the development of a plan to improve performance. Agencies can choose to use only the tools they wish and base their implementation plans on the information gathered by those tools. Once an agency starts to implement changes, the assessment tools can be administered again to check progress.

> More information on these assessment tools can be found in the APEX Guidebook series book "Applying the APEX Tools for Organizational Assessment," available at NIC's Information Center, *http://nicic.gov/.*

Other Quantitative Assessment Sources

Most correctional organizations use measurements to track and report on their performance, and many of these are excellent sources for assessing culture change readiness. One of the more rigorous sets of performance indicators is ASCA's Performance-Based Management System (PBMS). PBMS is a primary correctional benchmark for performance standards, measures, and common definitions of key indicators, with counting rules. Using it enables member agencies to compare "apples to apples" when comparing their performance on certain measurements with similar agencies. The *APEX Resources Directory Volume 1* contains lists of assessment tools for each of the APEX Public Safety Model domains and for change management.

Reviewing Previous Plans, Outcomes, and Audits

These types of documents were important at the time they were created and it will be useful to review them. Even though people often feel that the present is unique, much can be learned from the agency's history. The current culture, designed to perform as it is performing right now, was created by both current and former agency staff, structure, and culture. The review of previous strategic plans, goals, measures, outcomes, and audit results cannot be taken lightly. The results of these reviews should be documented.

Identifying Additional Information

Sometimes the qualitative review turns up some strong audit findings or a recent strategic plan that includes well-thought-out outcome measures linked to processes and results (such as a Kellogg Logic Model). There may also be a few gold nuggets among the best practices. Additional sources of information to consider include focus groups and surveys.

Focus groups. Focus groups can help meet two needs essential to managing change. They are a good way to connect with stakeholders to inform them and seek their input, and they collect subtle messages about where support and resistance lie. These are important because people support what they help to create; they like to be involved early on in a change effort, and the change management strategy needs intelligence. Some questions to consider in the stakeholder analysis include:

- Who are the most critical stakeholders relative to the planned change?

- Who has an interest in keeping things the same?

- Who has an interest in changes?

- Who will resist the proposed changes? Why?

- What is the priority order for communication with each stakeholder/group?

- Who will be supportive and willing to carry the message out to others?

Surveys. Surveys collect objective data, and they also tell stories and send messages, which are considered qualitative data. They can be used to gauge resistance, support, the magnitude of problems, and the sources of deterrents not yet identified.

Determining Readiness for Change

Readiness is defined as how prepared people and organizations are to take on something new, answering questions such as:

- Are employees open to new ideas and will they support innovations?

- How does previous experience with innovation affect the change now being considered?

- Will the change being considered create new requirements?

- Will internal or external pressures affect attitudes toward the potential change effort?

- What level of trust exists in the organization?

Most of the answers to these kinds of readiness-determining questions spring from the leadership style and philosophy of the agency and its senior team. If the senior team is open to an evidence-driven discussion about these kinds of issues, the organization is heading in a positive direction and toward an informed readiness assessment. Other considerations described below include (1) demonstrating leadership commitment, (2) garnering external support, (3) safety and security considerations, and (4) gauging agency capacity for change.

Demonstrating Leadership Commitment

Leadership commitment is critical to the success of any change effort; without it most efforts fail. Commitment is demonstrated through words and actions, such as providing resources to support the change process, demonstrating willingness to change personal behavior, building trust in the organization, or promoting a common vision of the future state embodied in the change effort. If leadership is committed, the entire correctional agency senior team plays an active role in communicating, directing, and championing this culture change. This means they must support and practice everything that is expected of the workforce. If senior management ignores the message in the vision statement, or "doesn't walk the talk," the change management initiative will fail and widespread cynicism will develop. The requirement for leadership commitment is simple: visibly engaged leadership 24 hours a day, 7 days a week. The same principle applies for the rest of the management levels in the organization. Middle managers and supervisors are just as responsible as senior executives and leaders for demonstrating that they value and support the change effort.

Garnering External Support

Correctional organizations operate as part of the larger environment in the public sector. Consequently, change efforts must consider legislation and regulations, political implications, governance structures, legislators, the courts, citizens, the supervised population and their families, the media, advocacy groups, labor unions, and the general public. Successful planning means determining how the change will affect different parts of the organization's external environment and identifying opportunities to obtain the support of these stakeholders. The consideration of external support for (or opposition to) the change effort should include a realistic and frank discussion about readiness. This is not a time to be artificially positive; instead, all stakeholders should look honestly at the whole landscape of problems and opportunities.

Safety and Security Considerations

A critical part of readiness for change in correctional agencies is to determine whether or not the agency is "doing corrections right." This means that the basic elements of safe and secure supervision and settings are in place and functioning well. These include:

- Management of public, client, and staff safety and security procedures.

- Management of individuals and populations under supervision.

- Management of control, operations, and security of correctional environments.

If an agency does not perform adequately in these three areas, the first steps on the APEX journey need to be identifying the gaps and dealing with the deficiencies. Once the agency is "doing corrections right," then further change can be contemplated.

Gauging Agency Capacity for Change

The APEX Change Management Model cannot work if the organization is not ready for change. Determining readiness for change will also help to manage the change effort in stages 2 through 6; however, in stage 1, "readiness determination" is just that. If the organization is not ready for change, the probability of failure is great. Unfortunately, an organization that operates in a transactional, low-risk, high-control culture is less able to confront the difference between current and desired states, and is less able to act rationally and use evidence and data for direction. For this reason, the change readiness decision needs the engagement of the entire Change Team, Steering Committee, Change Leader, and senior leadership in reaching a realistic consensus. Readiness considers the overall organizational climate for undertaking a change effort without hurting itself.

PREDICTING FAILED CHANGE EFFORTS

Most failed change managements happen in a predictable way: Management proclaims a change edict of some kind, posts a notice, announces it at an all-hands meeting, and expects it to happen. Middle managers and supervisors are left to figure it out on their own. Influential staff may not be in agreement with the change. Even if they agree, they may lack the experience, knowledge, understanding, or ability to implement the change. Middle management feels the pressure to perform the change from the "top" and intense resistance from their direct reports at the "bottom." This is not an especially fun place to be. Typically the change program flounders at this point.

When considering its organizational capability to make desired changes, an agency must ask the following questions: Are the staffing level, funding, and physical plant potential assets or deterrents, and to what degree? Are resources available to implement the change? Examine the workspace, equipment, technology, staff capabilities, and training. During a change effort, two types of work run simultaneously: (1) normal day-to-day operations and (2) change activities. Job roles may need to be adjusted, so an agency must consider the impact of this level of commitment. Many people (often the least dispensable and most important ones) will be asked to do double duty by working hard on the change initiative at the same time they are required to keep the operation flowing and to work on long-term transitional activities. Some people may temporarily work on the change effort up to 100 percent of their time, so their normal workload will need to be done by someone else in the organization or it may be outsourced. Basic skills training, space arrangements, technology, or equipment upgrades may be required. Part of readiness determination asks if adequate levels of support will be there when needed.

Is the senior team ready to stand together, and is the team committed to working collaboratively and moving the correctional agency forward? Is the agency "doing corrections right"? If either answer is no, more work is required to prepare for another run at the change effort in the future. An early answer of "no" is not negative, as it spares the organization embarrassment and disruption. In fact, doing nothing is a viable option and, in this case, failing at a major cultural change initiative is often worse than not attempting it. "No" means "not now," but it should also be a pledge to move the change into the future and then to create the conditions that will make change possible. If the answer is "yes," the organization should take the risk and move toward higher performance, and move to stage 2.

Stage 2: Define the Goal and Objectives

The second stage of the change management model documents what was done in the planning stage to define the goal of the change effort. Correctional organizations are almost always high-reliability organizations, so the change will inevitably bring some resistance. This makes it especially important to define the goal. Dig deeply to define the *primary* issue, problem, or situation that must change, as follows:

■ List the aspects and considerations of the goals and objectives of the change effort. Identify why change from current operations is necessary.

■ What does the new vision for the future look like? What practices, behaviors, processes, opinions, and results will change, and why?

- Who is affected? How will the change affect them? Whatever the focus of the change effort, whether it is internal to the agency or involves outside stakeholders, it will require changes in behavior.

- How will the agency know when the goals and objectives are attained? How will success be measured? Ultimately, success will be measured according to the completeness and sustainability of the change, so what will that change look like?

Express the change goal and vision for the future in a statement that can be understood at every level of the organization and by key stakeholders. This is the message that explains what is going to change and why it is important, in a way that is relevant to the agency's environment. The rationale for change should resonate with people both psychologically and emotionally as well as in a commonsense (program, business, legal, or regulatory) perspective. Data supporting a future need or trend that requires change are helpful here. Possibly a situation is brewing or is already out of control, which can help agency leaders demonstrate the need for action. A cause for change with a higher moral purpose, such as serving others better or saving lives, will generate stronger support than one that appeals simply to administrative necessity.

Clarify what is not going to be addressed. Determine what is negotiable (program offerings) and what is not (safety and security). The specific content of the change message needs to have "stickiness," a memorable quality that keeps it active in the mind. The message has to be worthy of passing on. Often the initial message has to be modified and repackaged before the right amount of stickiness is achieved.

Finally, the message needs to be simple enough to deliver in one "elevator ride." Creating this message is painstakingly hard because it must be perfectly clear. When it ends, the stakeholder should want to help make it all happen. More information on crafting messages for various stakeholders can be found in chapter 6: "Communications Planning during Change."

Stage 3: Organize for Results

Undertaking a major change involves the entire senior management team and the commitment of senior leadership, and completing it requires the engagement of not just one or two senior leaders but a team of people. Sometimes even minor change efforts will benefit from a scaled-down version of the roles of the Change Leader, Change Team, Steering Committee, and Intervention Teams.

Change Leader

The correctional agency's most senior official must take responsibility for getting the change done or delegating that authority to someone else. Sometimes the role of Change Leader is filled by the most senior executive in the agency. At other times someone is appointed to act as his/her alter ego, viewing the change with a different perspective and acting in the organization's best interest to allocate resources, negotiate with stakeholders, and manage the complex interactions that will occur. The Change Leader is the key staff person with the authority to implement changes; usually the CEO or director delegates primary responsibility to this person to help plan and orchestrate the change. This typically requires:

- Selecting the Change Team members or participating with the most senior leadership in team selection.

- Organizing the initial organizational assessments to identify strengths and gaps.

- Orchestrating the development of a plan to help the organization meet its goals and ensure successful performance improvement.

- Informing senior management of the status and progress of the change effort and ensuring their support to break down barriers, provide necessary resources, or reinforce communication.

- Challenging the management team when the evidence suggests that the process or any part of the organizational effort is faltering.

- Actively contributing to decisions affecting the organization.

- Providing guidance to the team on technical issues, quality improvements, strategies and methods, identifying consulting support, etc.

- Acting as a coach and confidant on behavioral and personnel issues.

- Managing specific projects that extend from the overall change management project.

- Proposing and organizing educational activities.

- Developing and managing a network that supports the change process.

- Advising the Steering Committee and seeking their support as necessary.

- Finalizing and adjusting the implementation plan.

- Managing the change plan and process.

- Developing action steps.

- Developing implementation strategies.

Change Team

The Change Leader needs an integrated team to support the effort; that is, a group of trusted minds who can do the analysis and, if necessary, the arm twisting—a Change Team. Members should be well connected, interpersonally competent, and diverse, representing different disciplines and levels in the organization. The team's composition may include clients/offenders, partners, community leaders, and those who are interested in and can impact success. The Change Team decides how the change is managed and who is involved in planning and implementation.

Their success requires time, flexibility, and control over priorities to operate effectively. The team is made up of people who can influence others and who keep the endeavor alive. They are trusted and respected, able to communicate effectively, knowledgeable about how things *really* work, familiar with the culture, and should have patience and persistence. Above all, each person on the Change Team must be willing to be changed personally. In his book, *The Tipping Point: How Little Things Can Make a Big Difference,* Malcolm Gladwell (2000) identifies three types of people who wield significant influence with others:

- **Connectors.** A handful of people who have an extraordinary knack for making friends and acquaintances.

- **Mavens.** These individuals spread the word throughout the organization about the change efforts because of their knowledge, social skills, and ability to communicate.

- **Salesmen.** These individuals have an indefinable trait that goes beyond what they say, which makes others want to agree with them.

Finding the 20 percent of people who can make 80 percent of the difference is the best way to get started. Identifying and engaging the connectors, mavens, and salesmen within the culture will take the change effort forward exponentially. As this group expands and exercises its considerable influence, others in the organization will follow, embrace the change, and make it happen.

The most effective Change Teams are not hierarchical; rather, they tend to follow a transformational approach to organization and leadership philosophy. Everyone has an equal voice as questions are debated and discussed. It takes time for everyone to express their concerns and ask questions. Evidence-based practices and data-driven decisionmaking are the rule, not the exception. Consensus should inform the rationale for change and the strategic approach.

In a large-scale change effort, the Change Team may be tasked with providing oversight and coordination of the Intervention Teams.

TIME MANAGEMENT

Wise leaders know that those involved in these change effort roles, especially the Change Leader, will need some time away from their usual duties to accomplish the work of the change effort. Time management can become a big problem if the Change Leader has a senior operations role such as a deputy warden/chief or above and some duties are not reassigned during the change effort. Time spent on the requirements of reflection, analyzing, planning, collaborative work, training, coaching, marketing, problem solving, brainstorming, conducting focus groups, and conducting interviews is critical to the success of the change effort.

Steering Committee

For larger change efforts that impact the entire organization, a Steering Committee is needed to support the Change Team and to be available to run interference if necessary. This is especially helpful when the senior management official is the Change Leader and the main champion of the change effort. The Steering Committee is often composed of managers from across the organization, labor leaders, and staff members who are influential with their peers and are considered informal leaders; it may include people from the county board, Governor's office, and key stakeholder groups (community agencies, advocacy groups, think tanks, academia, etc.).

Intervention Teams

Intervention Teams can be charged with different tasks. If a large-scale change is occurring, a number of Intervention Teams may take responsibility for researching and developing implementation plans in each facility or office, realizing one of the vision points that comes out of the larger change vision, or handling one of the objectives in the implementation plan. In a single-intervention change or when creating a change in one facility or for one policy, the Change Team may do the above tasks as a part of its work so there will be no need for an Intervention Team.

Engage the Change Team

These hand-picked individuals, known for thinking on their feet and operating with high levels of maturity, will model the way people should act when the culture change is finally complete. Managing them as a model team requires that they have clear expectations and goals with a minimal degree of oversight. This allows the Change Team to meet the outcome and results requirements set by the Change Leader and Steering Committee with as much creativity and innovation as the circumstances allow. When the change effort is aimed at increasing data-driven decisionmaking, evidence-based practices, productivity, creativity, and innovation, using transformational leadership practices with the Change Team is essential to avoid micromanagement—the antithesis of the change effort's aims.

The Change Team will usually require an exclusive, uninterrupted period of time to "gel," build, set norms, and plan. A 2-day offsite meeting with an experienced facilitator can jump-start this development. The team must determine its own meeting schedule and decide how it will communicate internally for project management control. Team members will need preapproved release from daily tasks. Commitment to this resource will serve the organization in the long run.

Change Effort Tasks

Among the tasks that the leaders of the change effort identified above must undertake is the development of a communications plan to publicize the effort to three groups critical to its success: stakeholders (both internal and external), managers, and employees. The communications plan should inform these groups about the change effort, address their hopes and concerns about the changes that will occur, and garner their support.

Communications Plan

Initial Change Team assignments often include the development of a communications plan. A stakeholder analysis (part of the communications plan) involves the identification of the entire universe of internal and external stakeholders who could be affected by the change and who could potentially have any interest in its outcome; it also involves choosing key stakeholder groups to focus on. Stakeholders can bolster the likelihood of successful implementation, but mishandling their influence can derail the effort. In this assessment, the object is to reach a subjective determination of each stakeholder's interest in the desired change result, the likelihood of support, and the message and resources that would be required to gain it. Detailed information on developing a communications plan and performing a stakeholder analysis can be found in chapter 6: "Communications Planning during Change."

THE IMPORTANCE OF SUPERVISORS

Internally, for most organizations, supervisors are the most crucial early stakeholder targets. Frontline employees look to supervisors for direction and support, and every supervisor should be engaged early on.

Dealing with Managers

Use an organizational chart to plan initial discussions with middle and upper management who are not part of the Change Team or Steering Committee. The Change Leader must be able to rely on this advice about whom to talk with and which individuals and groups will handle the interaction. Ideally, the conversation is best carried out by the person who has the most influence with each individual. In most cases, the immediate supervisor is best. Color code the individuals on the chart to show those who are expected to be or are already on board with the change, those who can become advocates with influence and education, and those who can potentially disrupt or delay the change effort. The Change Team should meet with the Change Leader and Steering Committee to discuss this analysis and plan for how to best deal with the possible detractors.

AVOIDING TORPEDOES

This may sound harsh, extreme, or even Machiavellian; however, it is anything but. Many a change effort has been torpedoed by a discontented manager. Negative influences must be taken into account and contingency plans to deal with these influences need to be set in place as part of a successful strategy.

Assessing Stakeholder Expectations

Once the stakeholder analysis has been completed by the Change Team, gather additional information from key stakeholder groups. For each group, ask three diagnostic questions: (1) What does high performance mean to this group?, (2) How would the group know and how would the organization know if it was a higher performing organization?, and (3) How would this change effort affect the group's expectation of high performance? These questions will clarify and provide input for issues such as why a change is needed, who will benefit from it, how the benefits will be measured, what will change, who will need to change, how the change will occur, and who needs to be involved in the change effort.

Encourage employee participation that keeps everyone engaged. This is important because evidence-based practices generate good ideas and pragmatic thinking throughout the organization. The goal is to encourage ideas from everyone at every level. Engagement builds buy-in.

Identify logistical and behavioral barriers and establish a contingency plan for effectively neutralizing them. The trap to avoid is the assumption that hope alone can be an effective change management strategy, allowing the luxury of ignoring pockets of resistance without developing contingency plans to address them. The Change Team is the primary advisor to the agency on anticipating and dealing with these contingencies. Typical roadblocks include lack of trust, low credibility, lack of a shared vision, inadequate middle management and supervisor support,

STAKEHOLDER ENGAGEMENT

As a part of the initial preparation for undergoing a major change effort, a correctional agency's Reentry Committee identified those in the community who would be impacted by the introduction of a comprehensive reentry program, including:

■ Nonprofit agencies that dealt with housing, employment, adult education, and human services.

■ The Departments of Mental Health, Labor, and Social Services.

■ The courts.

■ Local law enforcement.

■ Families of the clients/offenders.

■ Advocacy groups.

■ Volunteer groups.

A series of meetings helped to involve these groups in planning for the reentry program. Stakeholders were invited to help develop the vision of the new program and how it would operate. Establishing these engagements early in the planning process helped to generate good will and cooperation from all of these stakeholders, as they felt their concerns were ultimately reflected in the decisionmaking for the program. Both external and internal stakeholders realized that they were working toward mutual goals: successful transitions from the institution to the community and a safe and secure community.

These types of support efforts, which involve key stakeholder groups, can help an agency avoid surprises as it moves through the change effort, and can lead to the development of alliances that can facilitate and sustain implementation.

inadequate staff and organizational capacity, a political or territorial climate, ineffective sponsorship from the executive team as a whole, impulsiveness or lack of patience, ineffective communication, failure to commit adequate resources and time, failure to recognize and acknowledge positive behavior, and "double speak"—not walking the talk about empowerment or other professed agency behavioral values.

Stage 4: Build the Detailed Implementation Plan

The implementation plan is a detailed project management tool that is designed by the Change Team to help the agency manage and monitor project milestones and achieve the goals of the change effort. This adaptable plan should convey urgency, the kinds of innovation required, the level of complexity involved in thorny issues, and the sensitivities that are unique to the organization's environment or culture. An implementation plan needs to be designed in a realistic way so that it will help people throughout the organization clearly understand their roles and responsibilities during implementation and beyond.

CONTINGENCY PLANNING TO DEFLECT RESISTANCE

If change is not managed effectively, it is common to find passive and active resistance, incomplete implementation, workarounds, reverting to undesired behavior or the old way of doing things, low morale, decreased productivity, turnover of valued employees, disinterest in the current or future state, arguing about the need for change, absenteeism, and ultimately the failure of the change management effort. Careful contingency planning will enable the Change Leader, Change Team, and others engaged in the change effort to deal with obstacles as they arise and reassure all stakeholders that this change effort is solid and will be implemented effectively.

The development of the vision for the change effort gives people a chance to weigh in on the creation of a picture of what the new way of doing things will look like in the future. The clear definition of each point in the vision helps people see what they are working for, enables the Change Team to stay focused on the desired outcomes, and allows the agency to know when they have achieved successes (both in the short term and over time).

Different strategic planning methods are available for agencies to use to create their implementation plan. Key steps that need to be included are:

- Scan the environment to gain understanding of the forces in the social environment that can affect the agency and its change efforts.

- Learn from the organization's history and any previous change efforts to identify themes or issues that can affect the current change effort.

- Analyze the current state of the agency and begin to identify the practices, policies, and rules that are working well and those that are no longer needed, and where there are gaps that need to be filled.

- Create an agreed-upon vision of the most desirable future with a clearly defined set of vision points that describe what the organization will look like when the change effort is successfully implemented.

- Develop detailed action steps for each vision point, including who is responsible, resources needed, timelines, goals, objectives, measurements, and desired outcomes.

- Create a plan to communicate the implementation plan, its various action plans, and progress as goals and objectives are achieved.

- Engage others in the change vision and action plans for implementation.

Engaging leadership, staff, and key stakeholders in the strategic planning process allows diverse perspectives to be acknowledged, all aspects of the organization to be represented, and many voices to participate in the decision-making process as the implementation plan develops. A variety of participative planning methods can be used to develop the implementation plan, including the Search Conference (Rehm et al. 2002), The Conference Model (Axelrod 2010), Whole-Scale Change (Holman, Devane, and Cady 2007), and The Future, Backwards (Cognitive Edge 2006).

The objective of the plan is to provide a level of detail sufficient to manage the implementation effectively. Too much detail can stifle the creativity of those working on the implementation plan. The plan needs to be adaptable because it will change over time as the organization learns and experiments and as factors in the social environment (e.g., new legislation, change in political leadership) require changes. The trap to avoid here is losing sight of what the change effort is intended to achieve. The plan should keep that end in sight. Key stakeholders need to become advocates; managers, supervisors, and line staff need to get on board; progress needs to be communicated; and achievements need to be measured.

Stage 5: Implement the Change Management Plan

The implementation of a change management strategy that involves culture change is much like painting a building. Inexperienced painters might undertake their first job by slapping on a coat of paint and calling the job complete, only to find blistering, peeling paint on the walls after only a few months. They learn that front-end preparation is the key to success, that scraping to remove the old loose paint puts them in touch with problems on the surface that must be addressed before the final painting can begin. Further sanding and stiff brushing reveal more surface vulnerabilities that would have ruined the job if left unattended. When the seams are caulked and the surface is prepared with the correct grade of compound, then the walls can be primed and the painting can begin. If painting is a metaphor for APEX change management, the final paint application is the implementation step. If the front-end work was executed thoroughly, stage 5 is much like executing any project plan.

More information on strategic planning methods can be found in the *APEX Resources Directory Volume 1*.

In running the project, the Change Leader should rely on the Change Team to monitor and track progress on action steps. Failure to account for results will destroy a project. For every result there is an outcome that is made possible by an output, produced by a process or action, and fueled by resources (including people), which creates enough inputs to complete the activities. These action steps—each one leading to the next—should be anticipated and documented in the change management project plan.

Everyone in the agency should know where every phase of the change management effort stands. This is important for two reasons: (1) the entire organization suffers in the event of a failure in any Implementation Team and (2) everyone wins when everyone succeeds. Rumors carry the results of failures whether or not results are posted, so sharing all results is sending the message that data are highly valued and used. One way to communicate what

MOVING FORWARD

Some agencies create symbols of change that provide visual images to signify a new future. Others hold funerals to bury their old ways, honoring them for their contributions so that they can move on to reinforce the new future. Many successful change efforts provide people with "proof points" as soon as possible to validate progress, such as finding people who are doing small things right and crediting them to the change effort. As wins are gained, Change Team efforts expand toward progressively more difficult tasks and issues that begin to stretch and challenge people without overwhelming them.

is happening during a change effort is to create a scoreboard where progress and results can be posted for staff and others to see. Using a common scoreboard to display progress can help everyone see the progress, understand the challenges, and realize that success is occurring.

A vibrant communications plan is essential to keep information flowing during implementation. Messages that are tailored to each stakeholder group and their special needs will disseminate information about implementation quickly and effectively. In addition to communications between each employee and his/her immediate supervisor, other resources can be used to communicate with staff. Large "all hands" or townhall sessions, newsletters, announcements, opportunities linked to other popular activities, e-mail blasts, and letters personalized with office addresses or even home addresses are some strategies that agencies can use. The communications plan reinforces the "what's in it for you" message by targeting the specific message to each individual or stakeholder group.

The importance of communication—telling people why this change is happening and why it is happening now—cannot be overstated. People who clearly understand what is going on are less likely to resist change and more likely to accept and even embrace the change effort.

Once changes become a part of the organization's culture, they tend to stick. They are no longer considered "something new" but simply "the way we do things around here." The changes must be woven into the fabric of the culture to make them compatible with the organization's values and policies.

When the new way of doing things is outside of the agency's norms, values, or policies, these need to be examined and may need to be revised. If one of the values involves the maintenance of the status quo, changes will not be lasting. It may not be articulated exactly that way, but it will still have a negative impact. If an agency policy allows female officers to work with female offenders only, and one of the proposed changes is to match people's skills, abilities, and knowledge with their assignments, there could be a conflict with that policy. For example, the only officer in a facility who speaks Chinese may be female. If a male who speaks Chinese is incarcerated, she may be the only one who can communicate well with him. Through review, that policy could be rewritten to reflect the change.

Sometimes the old culture is not compatible with the changes. Even minor inconsistencies between the culture and the changes need to be dealt with before the new way of doing things can be fully integrated into day-to-day operations. Correctional agencies are known to come from a tradition of conservatism—changing slowly and with an aversion to taking risks. In today's correctional environment, the changes come rapidly and risks cannot be avoided, only managed. Many agency leaders have said that they would be more successful in their change efforts if certain people who resist organizational change would leave or retire. This is not unique to corrections. Companies in the private sector, as well as other public-sector agencies, have offered early or enhanced retirement packages as a way of reducing costs and moving staff out. This often makes way for new staff with attitudes that accept culture change. According to Kotter, "Sometimes the only way to change a culture is to change key people" (Kotter 1996:157).

Continuously adapt and modify the implementation plan. The change strategy was seen originally as a way to close a gap between the current reality of behaviors, culture, and operating practices and the desired state, a vision that became a shared vision for the future once this change management plan began implementation. To assume that the future can be predicted is to follow mindlessly along the lines of the original project plan. The only constant in a correctional operating environment is change, and it must be monitored and accommodated.

Stage 6: Sustain the Change

Sustaining organizational change depends on continuous reinforcement. Without reinforcement from executives, managers, supervisors, and other influential figures, the result is similar to what happens when a bicycle rider stops pedaling. Leaving the status quo for a new way of working is an uphill climb, and steep climbs need more intense reinforcement. This includes more frequent, closer, and more personally focused engagements, and increased variety in the way the reinforcement is conveyed. One trap to avoid is allowing a major change initiative to be seen as the "flavor of the month," a scenario too familiar to many who work in corrections and many other fields. The results scoreboard referred to in stage 5 can to be used to continually measure and post progress, demonstrating that divisions and subordinate units are accountable for their actions in meeting milestones and objectives. Other enhancements to sustainability are discussed in the following sections.

Integrating Changes into Cultural Norms

Changes need to be genuine and authentic. It is impossible to fabricate authenticity. The healthiest organizations are made up of adults who are able to enter into demanding interpersonal transactions, which is the most common ingredient in successful change strategies that integrate desired states into the culture. When this is working, individual actions and agency-prescribed behaviors are indistinguishable. The Change Leader, Change Team, Steering Committee, and Intervention Team often monitor this integration informally by listening carefully to discussions to identify when people are inferring that the changes are not being implemented authentically. They can also use more formal methods (e.g., focus groups, interviews, and surveys) to assess this integration.

Increasing Sustainability

Agencies that are successful in sustaining changes once they have been implemented rely on the following techniques: positive reinforcement of new behaviors, managing risks, keeping the pressure on through continuous monitoring of progress toward change, celebrating successes, planning for setbacks, engaging in ongoing evaluation and followup, analyzing performance measures and results, and adapting as necessary.

Positive Reinforcement

When the desired behavior is positively reinforced and the old behavior is discouraged, successful implementation is in process. Sustainability can be measured by the numbers of stakeholders demonstrating their support through actions, revisions to human resource policies and procedures that support the changes, and shifts in language (i.e., from offender to client or from jailers to correctional officers).

Risk Management

Risk taking is encouraged and carefully managed. A large part of the difficulty in managing and sustaining a culture change in a complex organization is the level of uncertainty that comes with leaving the known and moving toward the unknown. This is especially true in the high-reliability correctional culture, where to enter the unknown with open eyes demands that the most mentally agile employees risk, at least temporarily, ambiguity and disorder. If they are thinking people, this is inevitable. Major change makes it happen every time. Knowledge transfer begins with the employees who have the highest levels of mental agility and who can adjust to new situations quickly, pick up nuances, and translate vague situations into effective operating remedies. These are the key people who can make the change stick.

Monitoring and Creating Accountability

Monitoring and holding people accountable for policy, procedures, training, supervision, coaching, and stakeholder communication improves sustainability. Action plans for these and any other pertinent areas must be developed by the Change Team, with support from the Change Leader and Steering Committee. These plans are posted as action items on the common scoreboard created in stage 5, showing milestone dates, accountable individuals, units responsible for carrying out the objective, and intended outcomes or results for each item.

Celebrating Successes

Many of the requirements involved in implementing the change are important to sustaining it. Best practice research demonstrates that positive or negative reactions to events tend to be replicated in similar situations. Workforces with higher levels of (deserved) positive reinforcement will, especially over extended periods, tend to look for more ways to improve performance. Celebrating successes improves the organizational perspective toward culture and management change.

Planning for Setbacks

It is important to expect setbacks and recognize them as learning experiences and opportunities to reinforce the culture change as teachable moments. Do not allow a setback to derail the change project. Setbacks do not usually mean that the change cannot be achieved.

Ongoing Evaluation and Followup

Every correctional agency is a complex organization made up of hundreds of thousands of subsystems with thousands of variables that are constantly changing and placing demands on the way things function. Continuous improvement in this dynamic environment requires ongoing evaluation. The results of this evaluation will inform alterations in such areas as messages, stakeholder relationships, service contracts, communication strategies, operations processes, and security measures.

The kind of evaluation that applies will vary from one agency to another, and it is important to think carefully about how to choose and use this process. The evaluation may be developed internally, borrowed from another correctional organization and adapted for the agency, or adapted from one or more of the APEX Assessment Tools.

TAKING STAKEHOLDER TEMPERATURES

This informal evaluation method is meant to be administered one to one. It allows the agency to "take the temperature" of stakeholders about the change effort. A trusted Change Team, Intervention Team, or Steering Committee member (interviewer) sits alone with a stakeholder. After promising confidentiality, the interviewer asks three questions: (1) On a scale of 1 to 10, with 1 being absolutely the worst performance imaginable and 10 associated with celestial heaven, where does the organization's performance (or yours in some cases) stand?, (2) What is your reason for assigning that number?, and (3) What would it take to get you (or the organization) to 10? These three questions are repeated for each key stakeholder. The results are tabulated and combined to prepare a report that attributes no specific names but provides combined assessments from the entire population of interviewees.

SUPERVISOR POLLING

Another systemwide evaluation technique that can stretch the supportive culture is to poll the supervisors for the most flagrant behavioral violations of the change vision. The overall top five violations become the basis for feedback development projects to be completed during the year. Each supervisor and manager asks five peers several times over the course of a year about each of the top five behavioral violations and writes down their responses. The responses can be compared to see how they shift over time. This requires and builds trust, encourages a learning environment, and has a powerful track record whenever it is successfully completed.

Analyzing Performance Measures and Results

What good is a scoreboard if no one sees it? Post the data and invite analysis, both formal and informal. The analysis of performance measures and results as part of a change effort aimed at making the organization more positive should be a positive experience itself, one that creates opportunities for personal growth and organizational development. Informal analyses can happen at staff meetings or briefings, using questions such as "What do you think of the changes in absenteeism?" or "What effect is the decrease in violations having on your housing unit?" Formal analyses can be generated from information management systems or from ASCA's Performance-Based Measurement System (available through NIC's Information Center Library, *http://nicic.gov/Library/021116*).

Adapting as Necessary

Continuous scrutiny of the current state against the desired vision and its alignment with the organization's mission and values should result in constant adaptation to the stakeholder requirements, opportunities to improve efficiency, and workforce satisfaction. In addition, it should capitalize on the strengths of individual employees and minimize their weaknesses. As correctional agencies become adaptable and create effective change management processes, they are better able to sustain the change and find themselves well along the way to becoming both learning organizations and high-performing organizations.

SHARING LEARNING ON A NEW PROCEDURE

A group of probation officers was tasked with developing and implementing a new procedure for failure-to-report violations. Once it was put in place, the Intervention Team created a blog on the agency intranet for officers to post their experiences with the new procedure. Team members monitored the blog regularly and used the posts to capture information about what it was like to use the new procedure. The blog allowed them to take the temperature of the officers and supervisors on the new procedure. They posted reports regularly that synthesized all that was learned and led related discussions at staff meetings. The reports included changes in the number of failure-to-report violations prior to implementation of the new procedure and each month after implementation. This allowed the officers to track whether or not the new procedure was making any difference in their clients' behavior and the officers' ability to comply with their terms and conditions of supervision.

Exhibit 4: APEX Change Management Process Map

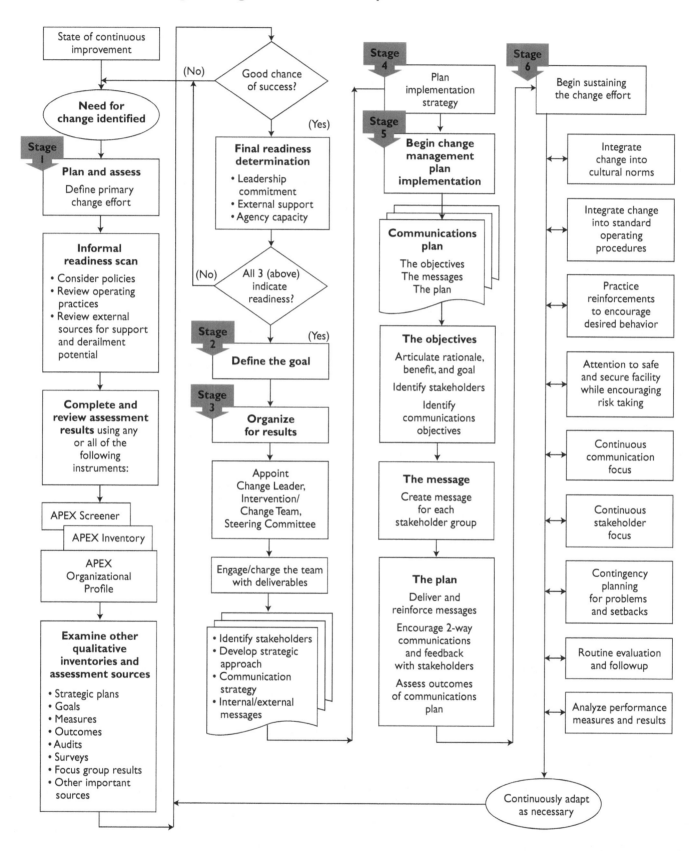

☐ The first symbol represents the fact that a correctional agency operates on the edge of stage 1, at the beginning of a change effort or near the end of one, signifying that the agency is continuously improving.

Stage 1: Plan and Assess

○ A need for change is identified and stage 1 begins.

☐ The change effort sets the course for the project management efforts to follow. It is important to understand what needs to change, why it is necessary, and what the change will impact.

☐ An informal readiness scan relies on several sources that are usually on hand to help assess the landscape of roadblocks and supports that inform strategy.

☐ Assessment results sharpen the organizational readiness picture. The APEX Screener, Inventory, and Organizational Profile provide a realistic assessment of the correctional facility's health and organizational readiness (fifth symbol and cluster of three below it).

☐ Other qualitative instruments sharpen readiness assessment and guide strategic direction. Possible sources are not limited to those suggested here.

◊ This diamond represents the first go/no-go decision point. A negative answer leads to aborting the launch to avoid disruption and, perhaps, another readiness check and examination of the issues that derailed the launch. A positive response encourages moving forward.

☐ This critical readiness determination looks at three factors: (1) commitment, including the key stakeholders in the entire senior team, (2) external support from stakeholders who could aid or derail the effort, and (3) agency capacity to complete the change initiative while maintaining a safe and secure facility.

◊ The last stage 1 event is a decision on a final "Launch?" question.

Stage 2: Define the Goal

☐ "Describe and Clarify the Goal" is informed by the work completed in stage 1. This exercise clarifies the change direction and finalizes the goal statement.

Stage 3: Organize for Results

☐ Appoint/assign the Change Leader to manage the project on behalf of the senior official.

☐ Identify members of the Intervention/Change Team and ensure that they have the vision, resources, and time necessary to get the job done.

☐ Identify the Steering Committee and ensure that they share the vision for the end state of the change and are prepared to give the project their full support.

☐ Engage the Change Team and Intervention Team with work assignments and organize teams, committees, etc.

☐ The next box represents documents that the Change Team should produce, including the formal identification of stakeholders; a strategic approach; a communication strategy; and messages to be delivered internally and externally that are designed to create awareness of the change and desire to support it, taking the special needs of each stakeholder into account.

Stage 4: Build the Detailed Implementation Plan

☐ The project management plan that formalizes work completed at the end of stage 3 is an outline of the Implementation Plan that provides enough detail to manage the change effort through implementation.

Stage 5: Implement the Change Management Plan

☐ This begins the work of implementing the plan.

☐ The communications plan includes developing the objectives, message, and plan.

☐ The objectives include:

- Articulating the rationale, benefits, and goals of the change initiative for the organization.

- Identifying all internal and external stakeholders who can influence the organization's success and their level of support for the change initiative.

- Identifying the communications objectives for each stakeholder group.

☐ The messages include:

- Formulating the message content to address the communication objectives for each stakeholder group.

☐ The plan includes:

- Delivering and reinforcing the message.

- Encouraging two-way communication with stakeholders, including feedback processes.

- Assessing the outcomes of the communications plan.

Stage 6: Sustain the Change

☐ Sustaining the change effort involves a number of subtasks, all of which are important, occur simultaneously, and contribute to the end state of continuous improvement by adapting practices as necessary.

○ Continuous adaptation to improve organizational performance, the end state of the change process, directs the path back to stage 1.

The transfer of knowledge to those who will be affected by the change effort is an important part of sustaining change. Outside stakeholders, other agencies affected by the change, clients and their families, and other criminal justice agencies are a few examples of those who may be impacted by changes. These stakeholders may not necessarily receive the same training as staff, but they need to learn about the change and how it may affect them. Active forms of knowledge transfer and communications such as blogs, meetings, and focus groups are more effective than passive forms, such as memos and letters. When multiple active methods are used, the integration of the changes is more effective (Fixsen et al. 2005).

Putting It All Together

Exhibit 4 presents the APEX Change Management Model in a process map format. It is complex and robust, showing how the systems approach to change management can be used as a roadmap for correctional agencies on the APEX journey. It begins with the discovery of the need for change and takes the agency through to implementation. The symbols in this high-level view of the change model represent activities, products, and outputs that may, in several cases, involve a number of steps that are not depicted. The notes following the process map explain the steps, symbols, and activities.

Summary

The APEX Change Management Model is a roadmap for successful organizational change. The six-stage process includes planning and assessment, defining goals and objectives, organizing the people in the organization to ensure the desired results, planning implementation strategies, implementing the plan, and sustaining the change effort. Strategies are provided for every stage, and a process map illustrates the pathway from recognizing the need for change through to successful implementation. The next chapter discusses additional elements that enable change.

References

Axelrod, R. 2010. *Terms of Engagement.* San Francisco: Berrett-Koehler.

Cognitive Edge. 2006. "The Future, Backwards," *http://www.cognitive-edge.com/files/Future-Backwards.pdf,* accessed December 2, 2011.

Fixsen, D., S. Naoom, K. Blase, R. Friedman, and F. Wallace. 2005. *Implementation Research: A Synthesis of the Literature.* Tampa, FL: University of South Florida.

Gladwell, M. 2000. *The Tipping Point: How Little Things Make a Big Difference.* New York: Little, Brown and Company.

Holman, P., T. Devane, and S. Cady. 2007. *The Change Handbook.* San Francisco: Berrett-Koehler.

Kotter, J. 1996. *Leading Change.* Boston: Harvard Business School Press.

Rehm, R., N. Cebula, F. Ryan, and M. Large. 2002. *Futures that Work: Using Search Conferences to Revitalize Companies, Communities and Organizations.* Gabriola Island, British Columbia, Canada: New Society Publishers.

Chapter 5: Additional Elements of Successful Change Management

uccessful change requires that certain elements are included to increase the chances of achieving the goals and objectives of the change vision and to enhance sustainability. Many of these elements are discussed in previous chapters. This chapter provides additional elements of successful change management for correctional agencies on the APEX journey.

Sense of Urgency

Change efforts in corrections have greater success when priority and pace are both organizational imperatives in the decision to embrace the change effort and make it sustainable into the future. This requires a constant drumbeat from the chief executive and the Change Leader, reinforced with the clear and obvious support of the entire senior team and everyone with supervisory authority in the organizational areas affected. One significant challenge is to keep the sense of urgency going during all stages of the change process, even when the agency experiences resistance, temporary losses in productivity, increased stress, and turnover. The steady drumbeat for action is a vital leadership function during change.

More on Determining Readiness

Readiness is an extremely critical issue when thinking about changing something in an organization. Taking the time to determine readiness, even before announcing the change strategy, seems obvious, but is often neglected or relegated to a cursory review. Correctional agencies can be driven hard to enter large-scale culture change initiatives before the resources, workload, financial capacity, and support systems are in place to make the transition. In one case, leadership commitment proved to be a major issue until a warden and a state commissioner personally took responsibility for this function. They made a full-scale effort to bring the facility's senior team on board so the leadership would appreciate the gravity of the problem and the need for a fast, responsive remedy that would have lasting results. The warden and commissioner were able to make the case on a personal level with every manager, emphasizing that if each one of them was not on board in reducing use-of-force incidents, the impact would reach them directly. These managers demonstrated they would support change by showing a willingness to dedicate time and resources to the effort.

Internal Capacity Assessment

Agencies that take the time to evaluate their internal capacity prior to undertaking a major culture change are better prepared to account for and to implement and sustain the change effort. Even more important, Change Teams are not surprised or blindsided by unanticipated events. The ability to create new policy and procedure changes is especially important because when changes are required, the agency requires the capacity to make them. Sufficient staffing needs to be available to address any shifts in workload. Training capacity, along with other resources, must be available. Another factor to consider is the internal capacity to handle strong community interest that generally accompanies a change effort.

Dedicate Time for Assessments

An evidence-based culture demands that assumptions and hunches are challenged so that decisions can be based on data and facts. It takes time to assess the organization's current performance and culture, review past performance, investigate best practices, and hear stakeholder input, but these efforts bring a wealth of information to the change effort.

Many correctional agencies rely on a variety of no-cost options, such as:

- The APEX Screener.

- The APEX Organizational Profile.

- The Organizational Culture Assessment Instrument (available at *www.ocai-online.com*).

- Best practice reviews.

- Reviews of previous strategic plans, goals, measures, outcomes, and audits.

In addition, interviews with clients and their families often provide qualitative information. Focus groups (of victims, supervising officers, correctional officers, case managers, clergy, employers, or any affected stakeholder group) provide an opportunity to discuss the problem, system considerations, root causes, and stakeholder engagement opportunities.

BEST PRACTICE REVIEW

One agency realized that there was a dramatic increase in technical probation violations impacting recidivism rates, straining the probation workforce, and damaging the agency's image in the community.

The Change Team and Steering Committee had already been formed when this review occurred. Two previously funded Pew Foundation nationwide studies of technical violation practices showed potential pitfalls and successful strategy choices. A review of the American Probation and Parole Association's measurement results identified several additional benchmark opportunities, which helped frame the problem in context for their situation. The Center for Effective Policy provided examples of successful probation and readiness practices in 16 comparable situations. The Change Team used all three sets of source material in the informal review before developing the detailed implementation plan in stage 3.

Organizational and Professional Agility

You can continually adapt to change or you can change to be adaptable.

—Robert Rehm

The only constant in the correctional operating environment is change. Therefore, it is essential to be ready to adapt as necessary. Agencies that are not constantly in a state of major adaptation tend to be those that enjoy strong stakeholder support, but even these organizations inevitably must adapt to changing demands, constraints, and opportunities. If a change requires a shift in operations or processes, having experienced a change management effort is an advantage. Building adaptable implementation plans allows for the inclusion of strategies to deal with possible constraints and potential setbacks. Including enough flexibility in timelines and resource allocation plans allows the agency to deal with unexpected occurrences.

As implementation proceeds, an organization should review and adjust the communications plan and action steps based on its progress, and should evaluate various aspects of the implementation plan or changes in the environment (such as new legislation, regulations, or case law). The organization should recruit credible individuals in the organization as messengers. Maintaining transparency about what is going well and what is not going well with the change sends a message of commitment for what is doable and for supporting words with action.

Stability among the ranks of senior management is desirable but not necessarily controllable. Having a succession plan for like-minded leaders to step in to keep the change effort alive is an organizational stabilizer. If a warden initiates a change process and then leaves the institution, those left in place should have been groomed to continue the process. This speaks to the value and prudence of succession planning to maintain and develop staff capacity at different levels—identifying change agents, giving them the tools to manage change, and educating them about sustaining change.

Understanding Individual Change

It is crucial to obtain help from all people who are affected by a new strategy, change effort, or reorganization. Individuals typically go through many stages during change, none of which is necessarily permanent. Elizabeth Kubler-Ross's (1997) stages of grieving include denial, anger, bargaining, depression, and acceptance. The following four stages, loosely based on Kubler-Ross's, help explain what those affected by the change may be going through:

1. **Denial.** The status quo is actually not so bad; the possible new way is threatening, unknown, and unproven. There may be a feeling that the change is temporary or not real at all.

2. **Resistance.** Do not want to change; do not want the pain. The fear of losing a job or changing work settings is strong.

3. **Exploration.** Openness to looking at new possibilities and alternatives without attachment. This is desirable and is usually present in more progressive correctional cultures.

4. **Acceptance/commitment.** Enthusiasm and passion for the change. This is a desired state.

More on Leadership

Correctional agencies that served as examples in developing the APEX Change Management Model often demonstrated this view of leadership. Leadership is what takes the organization safely from the status quo through a period of disruption to a better work climate and, ultimately, to a more positive organizational culture. A truly effective leader is an executive who has the ability to share the organization's values with more people than just the senior team. This kind of leader views leadership as a part of everyone's job. These exceptional executives and managers measure their effectiveness based on the degree to which the entire organization embraces and models the leadership messages on mission, vision, and values as they are carried out in strategies, structures, and systems throughout the correctional agency.

Leveraging the Supervisor's Role

The supervisor is in the best position to help employees accept change and do their individual parts to support implementation. Objective understanding of the need for change, the desired future state, and the advantage to the individual employee and to the organization in carrying out the change management effort is a message that the supervisor is well equipped to deliver.

Employee Role Alignment

Agencies subscribing to evidence-based human resources practices know that they must tailor messages to employees that demonstrate how their roles fit into the organization's larger mission, vision, and values. A change management effort goes straight to the heart of a vision's desired state. Successful change efforts engage all employees and allow for a discussion about how the changes will affect jobs, working conditions, evaluations, and roles.

The Supervised Population and Change

A key stakeholder group is the supervised population. Engaging them effectively at the beginning of the change effort will enhance the change vision, the implementation plan, and the sustainability of the changes. Individuals in this stakeholder group will have similar reactions to change that were mentioned earlier: denial, resistance, exploration, and acceptance. Many of the strategies presented in this book work well with these individuals. Openness about the changes, the potential impact of the changes on their situation, the timing of the changes, and other issues can alleviate potential resistance. Supervised and incarcerated individuals can provide quality input into the vision, strategies, and implementation plans, as well as feedback as the changes roll out.

Reinforcing Desired Behaviors

Desired behaviors are included in performance reviews during and after successful change efforts. This ensures that, at a minimum, employees and supervisors have scheduled conversations about these important subjects.

Public acknowledgment of positive performance can sometimes be an embarrassing but memorable method of reinforcement. Holding staff accountable when they fail to meet performance expectations also reinforces the change effort.

Dealing with Resistance

Some resistance is inevitable. A tension develops between those championing change and those seeking stability. Its evidence can be minor or explosive. Minor resistance can broadcast negative signals with damaging consequences, although even a small amount of resistance takes time and energy away from forward progress. Strong resistance is often rooted deeply in agency history. In these situations, patience, modeling adult behavior, and practicing empathy and tolerance are required to help people see things differently. This works best when the agency's cultural values are aligned with these practices.

Supervisors are key people in dealing with frontline staff resistance. An effective supervisor knows the strengths and weaknesses of the staff and dedicates planning and resources to maximizing the strengths of each individual and minimizing the impact of their weaknesses on themselves and the rest of the organization.

Many people are suspicious of change, especially at first. If the change effort is worth doing, then it is critical to develop and implement a comprehensive communications plan, including strategies to engage stakeholders. Well-crafted communications with key stakeholders, which address their expectations and needs, can shift resistance to "How can I help?" Following are some suggestions on engaging stakeholders and softening resistance:

- Explain what is changing and why in concrete, complete terms so that the sequence of events, timing, and desired end results are clear.

- Determine who will be affected by the change and anticipate their responses. Everyone needs to understand how the change will affect their jobs and the consequences of not going along with the organizationwide effort. Gather evidence from what people do and say to discover the *root causes* of resistance issues. This enables agencies to avoid dealing with only the *symptoms* of resistance.

- Choose the right time to begin so that people affected by the change are approached at their most receptive times. Effective pacing considers the daily workload and stress level of those involved.

- Evaluate and monitor constantly. Nurture positive changes and take swift action to address negative behavior and resistance fairly.

- Be prepared to make mistakes and deal with them as needed. Any resistance strategy is a trial effort, which means there will be a need to go back and adjust as resistance levels ebb and flow.

Another way to identify strategies to deal with resistance is to conduct an environmental scan focused on where there are individuals, areas, departments, or facilities that appear to be pockets of discontent regarding the change effort. Focus groups and interviews can help leaders understand the negativity. This can inform the communications planning so messages can be developed that target certain groups or individuals with similar triggers or issues, identify naysayers for inclusion, or assign influential people to help them see value in the change.

Proactive Handling of Critical Incidents

When a significant incident takes place and there is public outcry, stock in the change management effort drops. For example, a complex, multifaceted change management effort can come to a halt when someone on probation becomes involved in an incident that is on the front page of the newspaper and is a subject on the evening news. The result is that the agency has a negative public relations experience that lasts longer than is desired. Following are some lessons from APEX change management cases:

■ Avoid taking a reactionary, too-defensive posture.

■ Resist the impulse and political pressure to impose mass punishment.

■ Include a critical incident response in the implementation plan. This may include elements such as:

- Using leadership to set the direction and tone.

- Acknowledging the incident and its seriousness.

- Completing a thorough review of the investigation.

- Managing to address media exposure and political reactions.

- Reiterating the agency's commitment to public safety, e.g., "We will review our current practices to ensure we are maintaining public safety."

- Reassuring the public that the agency will take corrective action, e.g., "We will thoroughly review this incident and take corrective action as warranted."

- Communicating continuously and openly with the media, e.g., "We will advise you of our plans."

- Controlling impulsive action, e.g., "We are not able to discuss this incident while the investigation is ongoing."

Process Analysis and Positive Culture Change

Positive culture change is almost certain when undertaking process analysis and redesign work. The groups that are brought together to do this are often line employees, with few or no managers or supervisors. As a result, the line employees gain empowerment by making decisions about their work, processes, and outcomes. These groups learn about process analysis tools from the APEX Resources Directories and other sources. They find that after redesigning several work processes, they become skilled at this and often analyze and redesign, as needed, all of the primary operating systems in their units by following evidence-based and best practices. Their productivity increases as improvements are implemented, and this mindset expands throughout the organization as others in the facility see successes.

Emphasizing Ongoing Evaluation and Followup

Agencies that use data and measurement as a basis for their decisions tend to implement change faster and with less disruption than those that are not as rigorous about evaluation and followup. The evaluation process can be adapted to the original goal and milestone charts from the change plan. These goals and objectives usually include message delivery and desired end-state relationships, support required from each stakeholder group, and work completion milestones for processes and operations. Measures like these can follow the common scoreboard used throughout the change project, and they can be easily modified to become a reality check for the ongoing evaluation 1 year after implementation ends. Data on organizationwide impact objectives should be tracked at the agency level and updated monthly, which creates a continuous evaluation cycle.

Using the APEX Guidebook Series

The APEX Guidebook series was developed through the National Institute of Corrections to bring to the correctional field relevant information about a systems approach to changing organizations. The guidebooks are intended for people to use to inform, stimulate ideas, gain knowledge, learn how to effectively lead change efforts, assess organizational performance, and choose interventions to deal with performance gaps.

> The seven APEX Guidebook series books are available through the NIC Information Center at *http://nicic.gov/ Library/*.

Summary

This chapter provides additional elements to integrate into a change plan to ensure success. Taking the time to assess and determine an organization's readiness for change influences success. Also, planning to deal with the people involved—how capable the leadership is, how aligned the internal stakeholders are with the change plan, and how to reinforce desired behaviors and deal with resistance—is a critical component of a successful change effort. In addition, the APEX Guidebook series helps inform, guide, stimulate ideas, and assess performance for change. A communications plan is central to any change effort and is discussed in the next chapter.

References

Kubler-Ross, E. 1997. *On Death and Dying.* New York: Scribner.

Chapter 6: Communications Planning during Change

The development and implementation of a well-thought-out and dynamic communications plan is essential for the success of any change effort. The size and intensity of the change effort does not matter. Understanding the what, how, and why of the change effort; who will be affected by it; and its benefits and challenges is critical for success. It is not enough for the agency leader to deliver "the message"; internal and external stakeholders must be engaged in promoting the agenda.

What Is in a Communications Plan?

A well-thought-out communications plan includes:

- Objectives

  Step 1: Articulate the rationale, benefits, and goals of the change initiative.

  Step 2: Identify all internal and external stakeholders who can influence the organization's success and their level of support for the change initiative.

  Step 3: Identify the communication objectives for each stakeholder group.

- Message

  Step 4: Formulate the message to address the communication objectives for each stakeholder group.

- Plan

  Step 5: Deliver and reinforce the message.

  Step 6: Encourage open communication with stakeholders, including feedback processes.

  Step 7: Assess the outcomes of the communications plan.

Objectives

Step 1: Articulate the Rationale, Benefits, and Goals

First impressions are important, in change efforts as in other endeavors. Agency leaders, communications officers, and others identified by the agency need to develop an introduction to the agency's change effort. They need to make clear that "doing what we've always done" is no longer acceptable.

Rationale for Change

Clearly stating the reasons for change at the beginning of the process can do much to alleviate resistance later. Leaders in agencies that are embarking on organizational change need to be able to answer questions such as:

- Why does the organization value the change effort?

- How is this related to the agency's vision, mission, values, and strategy?

- Why are we doing this?

Benefits of Change

With all of the challenges confronting correctional agencies today, why begin a change process? Correctional leaders recognize that organizational change can lead to great benefits once they commit to the process of self-assessment and use the results to develop a strategy for moving the agency to higher levels of performance. Articulating the anticipated benefits helps stakeholders see how the change could make their individual situations better. Some examples of key performance outcomes that may result from a change process include:

- Increased facility safety and security through enhanced operations.

- Decreased staff turnover and absenteeism, and improved morale.

- Reduction in offender violence.

- Enhanced public safety due to increased offender success rates and reductions in recidivism.

- Improved communication with internal and external stakeholders.

- Enhanced data collection/information for informed decisionmaking.

- Demonstrated public confidence in the agency leadership and operations.

- More effective relationships with the media.

- More efficient use of fiscal appropriations.

Goals

Clearly stating the initial goals of the change effort helps people understand what leadership hopes to gain. Goals that are specific and measurable are an important component of any initiative. Examples of such goals include creating a policy for decreasing revocations, increasing staff retention by 15 percent, eliminating incidents of sexual misconduct, and lowering the recidivism rate by 10 percent.

Step 2: Identify Internal and External Stakeholders

Early identification of stakeholders and their positions allows agency leaders to develop strategies to increase stakeholder engagement and to begin to address any concerns, especially from those who are less than supportive. Stakeholder mapping is a useful tool for identifying the agency's stakeholders. Stakeholders can be sorted into groups by their interests and by the amount of impact they may have on the change effort.

A simple way to identify stakeholders is to have a brainstorming session and write down every idea identifying a stakeholder. The next step is to identify the most important stakeholders, i.e., those who could have the most impact on the initiative. Then they can be sorted into groups with common interests and/or traits.

Key stakeholder analyses determine stakeholders' attitudes toward the organization or the change effort. This type of analysis often looks at the type and degree of each stakeholder's influence and enables the agency leaders and/or communications officers to determine the type of communications focus that each stakeholder group will require (see exhibit 5).

Exhibit 5: Stakeholder Analysis

Stakeholders	Degree of Influence*	Communications Focus
Internal Stakeholders		
Staff	1	Engage and participate
Clients/offenders	2	Engage and participate
Middle management	1	Engage and participate
Labor unions	2	Engage
External Stakeholders		
Client/offender families	2	Inform and engage
Legislators	1	Inform
Other public agencies	2	Inform
Government budget office	1	Inform and engage
Private agencies	3	Inform and engage
Advocacy groups	3	Inform
Media	2–3	Inform
Citizens	2–3	Inform
Vendors/contractors	3	Inform

* Degree of stakeholder group influence: 1 = high, 2 = medium, 3 = low.

The thoughtful assessment of stakeholders and their degrees of support enable more focused communications objectives, message contents, and delivery methods. Strategies can be developed for each stakeholder group to most effectively use the agency's communications resources, depending on whether the focus is to inform, engage, and/or create participation.

Step 3: Identify the Communication Objectives

The communication objectives need to be tailored to each stakeholder group, depending on their level of influence, power, and support. Is the message intended to persuade, inform, educate, create participation, influence, change perceptions, influence behavior, engage, garner support, address concerns, or establish ambassadors to support the change? These objectives inform the content of the various messages.

Message

Step 4: Address the Communication Objectives

The message can be formulated, based on the stakeholder assessment and the identified objectives, to effectively meet the agency's communications goals and proactively address any issues and concerns.

A message designed to *inform* legislators, citizens, or vendors, for example, could read as follows: "Sexual misconduct incidents involving staff with inmate and inmate with inmate have increased 30 percent in the past 3 years. This behavior is contrary to the mission and policies of the agency, and it cannot be tolerated. It affects the safety and security of the facility, the staff, and the inmate population. The Prison Rape Elimination Act (PREA) includes standards designed to prevent, detect, and investigate any incidents of sexual misconduct inside correctional facilities. We will be implementing policies and procedures to increase the safety of all incarcerated individuals to comply with the PREA standards, and will enforce a zero-tolerance policy for any sexual misconduct in this agency."

A message to *inform* and *engage* client/offender families and friends could read as follows: "The Kerry Correctional Facility has implemented a zero-tolerance policy for sexual misconduct. We want to ensure the safety of all those incarcerated in our facility. We are working toward 100-percent compliance with the Prison Rape Elimination Act standards and will aggressively respond to any activity that may constitute sexual misconduct by staff or offenders. Please report any information that may involve sexual misconduct by contacting the Chief of Security or the facility hotline at XXX–XXX–XXXX. Our goal is to manage a safe and secure environment for those who work, visit, or live within the facility. Your support and assistance in our efforts are greatly appreciated."

A message to invite offenders to *participate* could read as follows, "The Kerry Correctional Facility has a zero-tolerance policy for sexual misconduct. All incidents will be fully investigated and corrective action will be taken against those who engage in sexual misconduct, including staff, volunteers, visitors, and offenders. Report incidents directly to staff or use the facility security hotline to report any issues or concerns. For more information, refer to your handbook or see your counselor."

A message to staff to inform them about how work will look during this process could read as follows: "As you know, we are working toward full compliance with the Prison Rape Elimination Act standards. There will be mandatory training on this critical workplace issue that will teach you about the zero-tolerance policy, procedures, and avenues to reinforce best practices in this area. Postings will be placed around the facility, including housing units, to ensure that all are aware of the expected behaviors and outcomes. As we continue toward our goal of zero incidents of sexual misconduct, the facility leadership will keep you informed as to our progress. Your input and feedback are welcomed during this transitional time."

Plan

Step 5: Deliver and Reinforce the Message

The communications plan includes multiple formats and opportunities to deliver the agency's message to its stakeholders. These may include one-on-one meetings, e-mails, website notices, postings, paycheck attachments, memos, letters, brochures, policy changes, media releases, videos, training sessions, newsletters, announcements during rollcall, staff meetings, and so forth. The message must exhibit the full support of the agency leadership and be reinforced multiple times in multiple formats.

Message delivery strategies can include:

- Conducting speaking engagements with external stakeholders (e.g., civic groups, criminal justice agencies, business leaders, community leaders).

- Meeting with leaders of public agencies.

- Meeting with media representatives (e.g., print, television) and inviting them to speaking engagements.

- Meeting with contracted service providers.

- Developing a video that promotes the change initiative.

- Establishing agency/facility committees to target performance excellence.

- Posting progress reports in agency newsletters, other media sources, and websites.

- Posting pamphlets and signs in facilities and offices to promote performance excellence.

Exhibit 6 is an example of message delivery strategies.

Step 6: Encourage Open Communication

Audiences need an opportunity to reflect on and respond to messages. Offering opportunities for feedback encourages support for and cooperation with the change efforts; it also increases interaction with key stakeholder groups. In the policy-driven world of corrections, staff and those under supervision need to have a voice in how they will work and live.

Exhibit 6: Message Delivery Strategies

Stakeholders	Degree of Influence*	Communications Focus
Internal Stakeholders		
Staff	1	Briefings from immediate supervisors, meetings, newsletters, rollcalls, focus groups
Clients/offenders	2	Unit meetings, postings, focus groups
Middle management	1	Meetings, newsletters, focus groups
Labor unions	2	Letters
External Stakeholders		
Client/offender families	2	Letters, postings in visiting areas, focus groups
Legislators	1	Meetings, letters, memos
Other public agencies	2	Letters, meetings
Government budget office	1	Meetings, letters, documentation
Private agencies	3	Letters, meetings
Advocacy groups	3	Letters
Media	2–3	Editorials, interviews
Citizens	2–3	Editorials, website postings
Vendors/contractors	3	Letters

* Degree of stakeholder group influence: 1 = high, 2 = medium, 3 = low.

The development of various formats to deliver the messages with ongoing reinforcement and repetition is critical. For the key stakeholders, one-to-one communication with the agency leadership may be the initial contact. Other formats, including memos, progress reports, newsletters, and public service announcements, can be used to reinforce engagement and support. Agencies should actively seek and respond to communications from stakeholders. Ongoing communication with stakeholders is critical; it enables them to provide feedback on what they hear and read and it will enhance support for implementing the change initiative.

Step 7: Assess Outcomes

Any well-planned initiative needs to have an evaluation process. Measures of success and outcomes need to be carefully identified, defined, collected, and analyzed. These outcomes and results inform adjustments and modifications to the communications plan.

If the goal is to gain the support of a particular group of key stakeholders, measures such as the type and amount of feedback or the number of supportive actions by the group (e.g., public testimony, media comments) indicate success. Stakeholders who become ambassadors of the change initiative demonstrate agency success in successful communication, stakeholder engagement, and feedback. The number of downloads of a website posting is one way to measure how many people are being informed about the initiative.

Sample Communications Plan: Compliance with Prison Rape Elimination Act Standards

How many times has a flawed communications strategy contributed to a less-than-successful change effort? In many cases, the development and implementation of an effective communications plan would have led to better outcomes. Correctional systems are under close oversight by the courts, regulatory agencies, and state and federal legislators, and are under scrutiny from the media and the public. Correctional organizations are expected to be effective, efficient, accountable, and transparent—all at the same time. This is no small task. The most successful agencies are those whose staff and leadership master a proactive and comprehensive agenda to address the expectations that stakeholders demand. Their work calls for performance excellence both in the daily administration of correctional organizations and in their communications efforts.

Developing a communications action plan will keep the initiative on track. Part of the plan is identifying the desired results and developing data analysis measurements so that actual outcomes can be compared with the desired results. A communications action plan may have several components to address the myriad activities. Exhibit 7 on page 60 aligns with the PREA compliance case study presented in the next chapter.

Exhibit 7 is an example of how one agency set up a PREA communications plan matrix:

Goal: Compliance with PREA standards.

Objective: Implement a communications plan to increase and ensure stakeholder support for the PREA standards.

Exhibit 7: PREA Communications Plan Matrix

	Steps	Actions	Responsible Party	Progress	Date	Outcomes
1	Benefits of PREA	Identify benefits and goals; report	Executive team	Executive team meeting scheduled 10/10	11/01	Report on benefits and goals by 11/01
2	Identify stakeholders	Conduct stakeholder analysis and force field analysis; report	OD director and management team	Meeting with eight managers as team participants	10/15	Report on stakeholder analysis and force field analysis by 11/01
3	Identify communications objectives	Review OD team report and develop communications objectives for key stakeholders	Executive team and PIO	Executive team meeting	12/15	Report on communications objectives by 12/20
4	Formulate messages	Review OD report and communications objectives	Executive team and PIO	Meeting scheduled	1/4	Messages to key stakeholders drafted
5	Deliver messages to stakeholders	Develop message content and delivery formats to stakeholders; deliver message to stakeholders	Executive team and PIO director	Message and format determined for key stakeholders; messages delivered	1/15	Messages delivered to stakeholders in multiple formats and schedules
6	Solicit stakeholder feedback	Hold focus groups; do surveys; conduct interviews	OD and PIO directors and staff, select managers and line staff	Continuous followup with stakeholders and requests for feedback	2/1	Stakeholders provide feedback
7	Measure and analyze outcomes	Develop desired outcomes; measure and report	OD and PIO directors and executive team	Report on outcomes monthly	Monthly reports on 15th	Outcomes support PREA Initiative

PREA = Prison Rape Elimination Act; OD = Organization Development; PIO = Public Information Office.

Summary

Once an agency's leadership decides to embark on a change effort, it is critical to develop a communications plan to ensure that the agency gains the support necessary to meet its goals and objectives. Without thoughtful planning and implementation of a strategy, the path to successful change may be met with resistance by influential stakeholders. With a solid communications plan, the agency will be able to enhance support for and success of the change management process necessary to sustain progress.

Chapter 7: Change Management Principles and Practices in Action—Prison Rape Elimination Act

This case study involves the fictional Correctional Detention Center in Kerry County (CDC Kerry), a medium-sized county in the American heartland. Kerry is a fictional county, but the story of this agency's change process comes from several of the best practices (and most challenging) cases that contributed to the development of the APEX Change Management Model. Following is an illustration of how one agency shifted its culture and organizational practices to implement the Prison Rape Elimination Act (PREA) standards.

CDC Kerry Change Management Process

The leaders at CDC Kerry chose the APEX Change Management Model (modified for the facility's particular circumstances) as the roadmap for changing the facility culture to full compliance with PREA standards. They wanted this change effort to be a systemwide endeavor to shift attitudes, culture, policy, process, programs, and outcomes. They realized that if it did not affect all parts of the facility, the staff, and incarcerated persons, implementation of the PREA standards would not be completely effective.

Stage 1: Plan and Assess

Assessing the Current State

The leadership of CDC Kerry was concerned about its compliance with PREA and the incidence of sexual misconduct and sexual assault among the detention population. The underlying cause for this concern was embedded in the facility's culture. By all outward appearances, CDC Kerry staff, as well as those in confinement, showed no signs of promoting or supporting awareness or commitment to prevent, report, detect, or investigate such incidents. When the detention population was assessed by confidential researchers and compared with other similar facilities, CDC Kerry fell in the top tier for incidents not reported.

This assessment also revealed a high degree of fear and perceived negative repercussions for those who reported incidents. As a result, the reported rate of sexual misconduct and sexual assault violations did not reflect the number of actual incidents and the failure to report incidents had not been officially recognized or addressed. The Administrator and Executive Team of CDC Kerry realized that this state of affairs could not continue because it jeopardized the safety and security of those confined and was contrary to the facility mission; also, the facility was not in compliance with PREA standards.

Assessments

The facility's Executive Team decided to use the APEX Assessment Tools Protocol, starting with the APEX Inventory and following up with the APEX Organizational Profile, to gain an understanding of the issues and the gaps in facility policies, operations, and culture that required change, and to identify and implement specific strategies to ensure compliance with PREA.

Through the APEX Inventory, leaders realized that CDC Kerry was ready for this change effort. Not only was it mandatory to comply with PREA standards, but many staff and managers were ready to look at what compliance would mean to their units and the facility as a whole. The team agreed that the facility had the flexibility, responsibility, and authority to establish systems, practices, and protocols that would eliminate sexual misconduct and abuse for those confined. Through informal assessments, a review of organizational documents, and interviews with staff, the Executive Team felt that some facility department heads, firstline supervisors, and line officers were reluctant to participate in this culture change agenda as it related to PREA. Many staff were uncomfortable with the mandatory reporting responsibilities related to staff sexual misconduct ("no snitching on other staff"). Others felt that sexual assault among those confined was an expected reality and consequence of detention; therefore, there was no need to take incidents too seriously and it was acceptable to speak about it in a joking manner. Without the commitment of everyone—from frontline staff to top management—the Executive Team knew the change effort for full compliance with PREA would not succeed. Staff and managers became one of the first stakeholder groups targeted in their communications plan.

Leadership Commitment

Leadership commitment to any change effort is critical from start to finish and is an important part of readiness. The Executive Team members made a commitment, individually and as a whole, to commit time, resources, and energy to implementing PREA standards.

Stage 2: Define the Goal

The facility Administrator and the Executive Team committed to an agenda to change the facility culture, enhance its operational procedures, and build and sustain a culture that supported sexual safety for those confined in the facility. The initial goal was to have an effective zero-tolerance policy and protocol that addressed sexual misconduct and abuse by staff and among those confined. The Executive Team's vision was for CDC Kerry to be a facility where attitudes, expectations, policies, procedures, actions, and responses aligned to prevent sexual abuse. The Executive Team realized that this would require fundamental changes in the culture, as previous efforts to implement PREA standards had not met the desired outcomes. They believed the goal of zero tolerance could be achieved while creating a sustainable cultural change that naturally supported the effort. Based on the APEX assessment results and the APEX Guidebook series, the Executive Team was better informed about what needed to change, how to implement the change, and what had to be done to sustain it.

Stage 3: Organize for Results

Identifying Affected Stakeholders

The facility Administrator and Executive Team were satisfied that there was support from the middle and upper management staff. Engaging others in the effort was now a strategic endeavor. The Executive Team worked with the managers and supervisors to develop a list of the frontline workers most affected by the change, and divided them into groups based on their behaviors, attitudes, work performance, willingness to adapt to change, and influence with each other. The Executive Team developed a plan for assigning someone to communicate with each of the staff on the list, just as the facility Administrator did with her leadership team; the intent was to seek staff input and support for the change effort related to PREA compliance. The plan included a strategy to engage those who were believed to be nonsupportive and possible strategies for involving the detention population.

Change Leader

The Administrator decided to name herself the Change Leader, with the full support of the Executive Team. PREA compliance was considered such a high-profile issue that having the facility's top executive as the Change Leader would tell stakeholders how much they valued the success of this change effort. Members of the Executive Team were available to stand in for the Administrator when she was unable to perform Change Leader functions. Providing backup in this way made it possible for the Change Team and other stakeholders to have access to change leadership. This meant that there was an increased need for communication and information sharing between the Administrator and the Executive Team.

Change Team

The Executive Team selected members to serve on a Change Team. Frontline employees, supervisors, midlevel managers, and administration staff across all facility disciplines and units were selected to be on the team, as was the newly designated facility PREA Coordinator. Each team member had perspective on the overall organizational culture, had demonstrated a willingness to work for progress and change, and had personal power and influence within the facility. All of the team members were invited to a meeting with the Change Leader and the Executive Team to learn about their charge and scope of work. The Change Team members were granted normal work time and/or were compensated to do this important work. During this change effort, the team members reported regularly to the Change Leader and Executive Team. They were held accountable for developing the change effort plan and for identifying strategies to implement the plan. Facility leadership committed to invest in the resources that the Change Team required and to provide support and guidance to the team as needed.

Engaging the Change Team and Building Capacity for Success

The new Change Team met to set ground rules for how the team would perform and conduct meetings. The members agreed that everyone was equal on this team and that it was a safe place to express ideas and disagreements. The PREA Coordinator educated the team on the PREA standards. Members of the Executive Team attended meetings to affirm the Change Team charter, share the APEX assessment results, and participate in targeted discussions, including:

- Why change?

- Where do we want to go?

- How do we get there?

- Who are our stakeholders and what roles do they play?

- How do we sustain our change?

The Change Team met regularly and developed an implementation plan with short- and long-term action goals. These goals included enhancements in policy and procedures, staff training, PREA presentations for the detention population, investigations, responses to those who report incidents, and supervisory responsibility to reinforce compliance with PREA standards. The team researched best practices for PREA compliance across the country. They developed a strategy to measure the success of the goals and to measure and analyze incidents involving sexual misconduct. They also developed performance measures to determine the successful integration of PREA compliance into the agency culture.

Implementing the Communications Plan

The Change Team decided to follow the recommendations in the National Institute of Corrections' APEX Initiative for developing and implementing a communications plan (see exhibit 7 in chapter 6 for details).

The plan addressed the *objectives* of the change issue, including the need, rationale, benefits, and goals of the change initiative; identified internal and external stakeholders who could influence the successful integration of PREA and their level of support; and identified the communication objectives for each stakeholder group. The Change Team formulated the *message* content to address the communication objectives for each stakeholder group. With the message content defined, the team developed the action *plan* to deliver and reinforce the message; encouraged open communication with stakeholders, including specific avenues for feedback; and identified means to assess the outcomes of the communications plan for change and the desired future workplace culture. The team members focused on creating urgency among staff for the change to full PREA compliance and ways to raise awareness and commitment among the detention population. The Change Team developed a focused PREA message that supported the facility mission and policies, including the key values, desired goals, behavioral principles, and expectations that defined the organizational culture around creating a safe and secure environment that was free from incidents of sexual misconduct.

The communications strategy included influential staff who were charged with providing examples of incidents or events that illustrated the key values for a healthy culture free of sexual abuse. These examples and stories articulated the desired vision for the future and added clarity to the mission-critical goal of staff and inmate safety. Using these stories in training sessions with all staff reinforced their responsibilities regarding zero tolerance of sexual misconduct. Orientation of newly committed offenders to the detention facility included stories to reinforce that the facility ensured a safe reporting culture to address any issues of sexual misconduct or assault. Displaying posters that reinforce a reporting culture in the staff areas and in the housing units also served to reinforce the zero-tolerance policy.

Stage 4: Build the Detailed Implementation Plan

The Change Leader (Administrator) and the Executive Team discussed the vision for change with department heads and middle managers and enlisted their support in the change process. The Administrator directly tied the benefit of the change activities to the success of the facility's mission and values and discussed PREA's legal ramifications as well as the responsibility of all staff to support the safety and well-being of the detention population. All managers and supervisors were invited to express their concerns, their questions were answered, and, most important, they were encouraged to offer suggestions and ideas for implementing and sustaining full PREA compliance. Sample communication documents are included at the end of this chapter.

The Change Team reviewed the information that had been gathered earlier (in the plan and assess stage) to help them develop an implementation strategy and change plan. The plan was communicated to all staff and other stakeholders and offered many opportunities for people to get involved through feedback sessions, planning for specific interventions, and committee membership to review a variety of policies and practices that were impacted by PREA standards.

Stage 5: Implement the Change Management Plan

The Change Team monitored and tracked the progress on the action steps and the implementation timeline. A PREA compliance scoreboard was developed and displayed in the facility, and it was updated regularly. The Change Team shared this information with key stakeholder groups through a variety of methods recommended in the communications plan. They worked with frontline supervisors to keep abreast of line staff's concerns and successes. As challenges arose, they worked with the Change Leader and Executive Team to address those challenges quickly. As the implementation continued, strategies to deal with resistance included openly communicating about how the changes were working, scanning the organization and its environment to check for tension or discontent with the new policies and practices, and willingly admitting that some things did not work as expected and revising them so they would be more effective.

Stage 6: Sustain the Change

To sustain PREA compliance as a facility priority, managers and supervisors became responsible for discussing the issue regularly with staff in meetings and for reinforcing it continuously with the incarcerated population. All staff were viewed as part of the Change Team efforts. Everyone in the facility became aware of the true meaning of a zero-tolerance policy. The Executive Team publicly recognized staff who were doing things right or making positive changes. Staff who did not abide by the performance expectations and violated the policy or law received timely discipline and/or corrective action in a prescribed and appropriate manner. The reporting of sexual misconduct by the detention population increased after the change efforts were initiated, illustrating a growing confidence among the detention population that sexual misconduct would be addressed by the administration. The PREA Coordinator regularly met with small groups of staff and the detained population to gather feedback, take the pulse of the change effort outcomes, and monitor progress. Any feedback, including that provided in staff training sessions or in meetings with the detention population, was shared regularly with the Executive Team. In addition, feedback was provided to all staff on the facility's compliance with PREA standards through the scoreboards, briefings, the intranet, and through other means.

Evaluating Facility Success

Because of the cultural and organizational change efforts, CDC Kerry achieved successful compliance with PREA standards at its next assessment. The facility established an ongoing systemic process to assess and adjust policies, practices, and allocation of resources to address problems; reinforce a zero-tolerance policy; and support a reporting culture. In addition, the facility enhanced safety and security while achieving greater transparency of the facility's sexual abuse data and efforts to prevent, detect, and respond to sexual abuse. Staff at CDC Kerry now believe that PREA is not just a set of standards, but a core responsibility for everyone in the facility. Detainees say they are now confident that staff will appropriately respond if they report an incident of sexual misconduct. Because of the PREA change effort, staff appear to be more comfortable with change and engage more appropriately on sensitive issues with each other, the administration leaders, and the detention population.

Sample Documents

The following documents are presented as examples of what an agency might include as a part of its communications plan for implementing PREA standards compliance.

Objectives

Step 1: Articulate the rationale, benefits, and goals of the change initiative.

Step 2: Identify all internal and external stakeholders who can influence the organization's success and their level of support for the change initiative.

Step 3: Identify the communication objectives for each stakeholder group.

Message

Step 4: Formulate the message to address the communication objectives for each stakeholder group.

Plan

Step 5: Deliver and reinforce the message.

Step 6: Encourage open communication with stakeholders, including feedback processes.

Step 7: Assess the outcomes of the communications plan.

Goal

Implement Prison Rape Elimination Act (PREA) standards at CDC Kerry to enhance safety and security.

Actions

■ Have the Executive Team review and indicate their support for the PREA change initiative.

■ Identify and analyze current data on sexual assault incidents.

■ Establish a Change Team to do the following:

• Review PREA standards.

– Contact the National Institute of Corrections (NIC).
– Review other jail models.

• Train key staff on PREA standards.

– Contact the NIC Jails Division.

• Ensure that facility policies and procedures are in compliance with PREA standards.

• Develop staff training lesson plans that include stories about victims of sexual abuse and the consequences for staff who engage in sexual misconduct; include examples of appropriate staff responses and positive effects on facility culture, and emphasize enhanced safety and security with the new policy.

• Revise the inmate orientation process and Inmate Handbook; use NIC materials, videos, and stories to illustrate the importance of the issue.

• Develop a communications plan that encompasses the following:

– Articulate the rationale, benefits, and goals of enforcing PREA standards for the facility.
– Identify all internal and external stakeholders who can influence the facility's success and their level of support for PREA.
– Identify the communication objectives for each stakeholder group.
– Formulate the message content to address the communication objectives for stakeholder groups to inform and engage them in the PREA initiative.
– Deliver and reinforce the message in multiple formats.
– Encourage open communication with stakeholders and create feedback processes.
– Assess the outcomes of the communications plan.

Specific activities to meet the above seven steps may include:

– The Administrator writes a memo to all staff to announce efforts and expectations.
– The Administrator writes a followup memo to announce the policy, identify the PREA Coordinator, and implement activities.
– The committee chair (Chief of Security) attends rollcalls and staff meetings to provide updates.
– Members of the PREA Change Committee spread the word at staff meetings and respond to issues, concerns, and questions.

- Develop posters that address staff misconduct and consequences.
- Conduct townhall meetings.
- Post information in housing units.
- Provide access to a community advocacy group.
- Acquire and post literature and posters for offender awareness and reinforce reporting methods, including confidential phone numbers for contacts.
- The Administrator discusses the initiative informally with legislators.
- The Committee Chair reaches out to advocacy groups that work with sexual assault victims for input, support, and collaboration regarding policy implementation and methods for offenders to report concerns.

- Monitor policy implementation.

- Develop a reporting and analysis system for incidents.

- Identify a PREA Coordinator to coordinate all activities related to compliance.

- Establish a Sexual Assault Response Team (SART).

The permanent PREA Coordinator and SART members sustain communication and implementation efforts with the Executive Team, facility staff, and offenders. Activities include the following:

■ Analyze PREA-related incidents for process/performance improvement.

■ Incorporate the new policy and results into facility newsletters and the annual report.

■ Stay focused and remain committed to the issue; stay the course.

To: CDC Kerry Staff

From: CDC Kerry Administrator

Subject: Sexual Safety of the Offender Population

One of the challenges facing correctional systems nationally, including CDC Kerry, is the incidents involving sexual abuse of incarcerated offenders. The purpose of this memo is to reinforce the duty of all staff, volunteers, contractors, and visitors to report any information or knowledge related to sexual abuse of offenders, and to establish a firm zero-tolerance policy related to sexual abuse.

The mission of CDC Kerry is to protect the public and ensure a safe environment for staff and offenders. It is our responsibility and obligation to do our best to prevent, detect, report, respond to, and address incidents of sexual abuse. Any incident of sexual abuse among those who are under our custody and care is a violation of our facility mission, our policies and procedures, our ethics, and our values as professionals in the correctional field.

Our efforts to eliminate sexual abuse are informed by the U.S. Department of Justice Prison Rape Elimination Act (PREA) draft standards for correctional facilities. I have established a multidisciplinary committee, under the leadership of the Chief of Security, to review these standards and add to or modify our facility policy and procedures for compliance. We will enhance and expand our training of staff, volunteers, and contractors regarding this subject to ensure that all who have regular contact with the offender population are informed and aware of the zero-tolerance policy, accountability, and response and performance expectations. In addition, inmate orientation and the Inmate Handbook will be revised to more clearly define this subject and provide avenues for those in our custody to safely report incidents of sexual abuse.

In the coming weeks, you will be receiving updates from senior leaders on our progress as we dedicate ourselves to an operational environment and facility culture that support staff professionalism and enhance overall facility security and safety for both staff and offenders.

Sample Document 4: Staff Rollcall, Newsletter, or Posting Memo— Update on PREA Efforts

To: CDC Kerry Staff

From: CDC Kerry Administrator

Subject: Sexual Safety of the Offender Population

A few months ago, I wrote to you regarding our efforts to reinforce our policy and procedures related to the sexual safety of offenders. I wish to update you on the great progress we are making with this critical safety and security issue.

Under the leadership of the Chief of Security, the multidisciplinary committee has developed a comprehensive policy that addresses our commitment to zero tolerance of sexual abuse and provides procedures and expectations that will define our response. I have approved this policy and have requested that it be posted and delivered to each staff member with signed confirmation of receipt. In addition, lesson plans have been developed that will serve to train staff, volunteers, and contractors who have direct contact with the offender population.

The inmate orientation process and the Inmate Handbook have been revised to emphasize our zero-tolerance policy and inform the offender population of the new policy directive, procedures, and practices. Staff who conduct offender orientation will receive individual training on the Prison Rape Elimination Act (PREA) standards, the specifics of the new policy, the effects on the offender population, and how to communicate the policy and procedures to the offender population to support and enhance the reporting of any concerns related to sexual abuse. Facility staff will also receive a copy of the revised Inmate Handbook for reference purposes. Rollout of the enhanced inmate orientation process and Inmate Handbook will commence 2 weeks after staff have received the new policy. During that time, staff will have an opportunity to ask questions.

For ongoing support of the policy, procedures, and efforts at eliminating sexual abuse, I have identified a dedicated PREA Coordinator, Captain Smith, who will coordinate all activities related to the new Sexual Assault Prevention and Intervention Policy. He will also serve as the Chair of the Sexual Assault Response Team. Captain Smith has recently received training on PREA standards through the National Institute of Corrections, and we are already reaping the benefits of his expertise in this subject. Any specific questions may be referred to him.

I am confident that when policy and procedures are understood, staff training is enhanced, and the offender population knows that sexual abuse will not be tolerated and they can expect a measured and appropriate response, we will dramatically improve the safety and security of our facility. Our integrity is based on how we dedicate ourselves to our mission of public safety, staff safety, and a safe and secure environment for offenders. It is with great pride that I work with you, the dedicated staff, to meet our mission.

Policy. The Kerry County CDC shall maintain a zero-tolerance policy on sexual abuse and sexual assault that actively identifies and monitors any inmate who exhibits characteristics of a victim or predator. All staff, volunteers, and contractors shall report any information related to sexual abuse in a timely and appropriate manner.

1. **Authority and Reference**

   - Public Law 108–79, Prison Rape Elimination Act (PREA) of 2003.

   - American Correctional Association, *Standards for Adult Correctional Institutions, Fourth Edition,* 2003, Standards 4–4281–1 through 4–4281–8 and 4–4406.

   - American Correctional Association, *Performance-Based Standards for Adult Local Detention Facilities, Fourth Edition,* 2004, Standards 4–ALDF–2A–29, 4–ALDF–4D–22, 4–ALDF–4D–22–1 through 4–ALDF–4D–22–8, and 4–ALDF–7B–10.

   - National Commission on Correctional Health Care, *Prison Health Standards,* 2003, Standard P–G–09.

   - State statute on sexual assault.

2. **Definitions and Acronyms.** For the purposes stated herein, the following definitions and acronyms apply:

   Abusive Sexual Contact. The intentional touching, either directly or through the clothing, of the genitalia, anus, breasts, inner thigh, or buttocks of another person without his or her consent, or of a person who is unable to consent or refuse. Abusive sexual contact shall also include any unwanted and/or forced kissing and hugging.

   HIV. Human Immunodeficiency Virus.

   Nonconsensual Sexual Act. The intentional contact between the penis and the vagina or the penis and the anus including penetration, however slight; OR contact between the mouth and penis, vagina, or anus; OR penetration of the anal or vaginal opening of another person by a hand, finger, or another object without his or her consent, or of a person who is unable to consent or refuse.

   PBMS. Performance-Based Measurement System.

   PREA Coordinator. Designated staff person who is knowledgeable regarding the Prison Rape Elimination Act and its standards.

   Separation Profile. A record specifying the need and reason for keeping two or more individuals apart from each other.

   Sex Offender Programs. Services that may include orientation, psychoeducational groups, individual counseling, group counseling, pharmacological interventions, discharge planning, and other clinical interventions.

Sexual Assault. For the purposes of this Directive, sexual assault shall be a collective term encompassing the definitions of Abusive Sexual Contact, Nonconsensual Sexual Act, Staff Sexual Harassment, and/or Staff Sexual Misconduct.

Staff Sexual Harassment. Any behavior or act of a sexual nature directed toward an inmate by an employee, volunteer, official visitor, or other agency representative, to include unlawful sexual relationships of a romantic nature between staff and inmates.

Staff Sexual Misconduct. Behavior that includes repeated verbal statements, comments, or gestures of a sexual nature to an inmate by an employee, volunteer, official visitor, or other agency representative.

3. **Staff Training.** Each employee, volunteer, and contractor who comes into direct contact with inmates shall receive training in sexual assault prevention, the zero-tolerance policy regarding sexual abuse, and related topics in accordance with this policy.

Preservice Orientation Training. Newly hired staff with direct inmate contact shall receive training on sexual assault prevention and the zero-tolerance policy regarding sexual abuse prior to being assigned to a facility post. Staff shall be trained to:

- Have a general understanding of PREA.
- Identify sexual assault as it occurs in jails and prisons.
- Identify the traits and characteristics of the potential victim.
- Identify the traits and characteristics of the potential predator.
- Identify rape trauma syndrome.
- Identify staff intervention practices.
- Discuss the crime scene preservation protocol for sexual assault.

Inservice Training. Staff with direct inmate contact shall receive refresher training on sexual assault prevention annually. This training shall include issues related to cultural awareness, responsibilities for reporting sexual abuse, consequences for engaging in behavior that violates this policy, and other specialized training as appropriate.

Rollcall Notices. The facility shall update staff as needed via rollcall notices as directed by the facility Administrator.

4. **Inmate Orientation.** Each inmate, upon admission to the Kerry County CDC, shall receive orientation that includes a presentation of the "Sexual Assault Prevention for Inmates" video. Each inmate shall sign the designated form acknowledging receipt of sexual assault materials, including the "Sexual Assault Prevention for Inmates" brochure, the Inmate Handbook with information regarding PREA, the zero-tolerance policy for sexual abuse, avenues to report sexual abuse, access to confidential counseling and reporting to an outside advocacy group, and a means to report any issues related to personal safety. In addition, upon admission, the orientation/unit counselor shall meet with each inmate to familiarize him/her with the written orientation materials.

5. **Victim Profile.** The following represents characteristics or traits that may subject an inmate to sexual assault:

- Vulnerable.
- Nonviolent.
- Young or youthful in appearance.
- Small physical stature.
- First time incarcerated or new to the facility.
- Effeminate (e.g., beardless, smooth skinned, more feminine in appearance).
- Gay, lesbian, bisexual, and/or transgender.
- Engaging in promiscuous or provocative behavior.
- Lacking street smarts.
- Mental illness or intellectual disability/deficit.
- Physical disabilities.
- Past victim of sexual assault.
- Convicted of a sex crime.

It is important to note that the above list is not all-inclusive and an inmate may not exhibit any of the traits listed above prior to an incident of victimization.

6. **Predator Profile.** The predator in a male-on-male or female-on-female sexual assault does not necessarily perceive himself/herself as being homosexual. Often, the perpetrator is hypermasculine and uses aggression to gain a sense of importance. The sexual predator will watch and wait until the right type of inmate is accessible and will create an opportunity to begin the "grooming" of the targeted inmate. The typical predator may demonstrate one or more of these character traits:

- Violent history (street smart and an experienced fighter).
- History of sexually assaulting other inmates.
- History of being sexually assaulted.
- Large physical stature.
- Mentally challenged.
- Possesses power and authority (feared by most inmates and staff).
- Recidivist (experienced in prison culture).
- Antisocial personality.
- More verbal, aggressive, and extroverted (extremely self-confident).
- Manipulative.
- Engages in other criminal activity.

- Objectifies women (uses pornography personally, as well as using it to barter with and to manipulate other inmates).

7. **Staff Awareness.** Staff awareness is an important component for curtailing sexual assault. Staff shall focus on identifying potential signs of victimization and intervene before the incident occurs. Staff shall treat any observation of sexual activity as a potential sexual assault. Staff may gain awareness through:

- The discovery of a sexual assault in progress or the observation of an incident, which includes sexual threats or pressure.
- A victim's report of an incident that has occurred.
- Information provided by a third party, i.e., another inmate, family member, or advocacy group member.
- The discovery of medical evidence of a sexual assault during an examination.
- Overhearing inmates discussing an incident involving sexual assault.
- Unlikely friendships that develop that raise curiosity, such as an older, more experienced inmate befriending a younger, less experienced inmate.
- An inmate displaying some of the characteristics of rape trauma syndrome:
  - Sleep difficulties.
  - Disturbed eating habits.
  - Symptoms specific to the attack.
  - Startled reactions.
  - Withdrawn.
  - Emotional expressions such as crying or shaking.
  - Isolates from others.
  - Extremely overalert.

An inmate may fit some of the characteristics associated with the victim profile.

8. **Sexual Assault Prevention**

On Intake to the Facility. During intake, staff shall conduct screening to inform appropriate housing, bed, work, education, and program assignments, and shall determine through the appropriate classification means if a victim/predator profile exists. If a victim/predator profile exists, the staff member discovering the profile shall verbally report the profile to the shift commander or designee to inform appropriate housing assignments.

While Housed at the Facility. Staff shall conduct random tours throughout their area(s) of responsibility in accordance with facility policy "Tours and Inspections." Video surveillance cameras shall be used to augment staff tours for increased observation. In each area of the facility, staff shall identify blind spots where sexual assaults are at higher risk of occurring and develop a strategy to compensate for such areas in accordance with the PREA Coordinator and Chief of Security.

9. **Staff Monitoring and Intervention.** All staff, volunteers, and contractors shall report any instance of alleged or actual sexual assault/victimization to a shift supervisor as soon as practical and provide documentation in accordance with facility policy "Reporting of Incidents." Failure to report may subject the individual to discipline, up to and including dismissal.

Staff Action. If a staff member suspects or an inmate alleges that he/she or another inmate may have suffered a sexual assault or victimization, the following actions shall be implemented:

- Identify, separate, and secure the inmates involved.
- Identify the crime scene and maintain the integrity of the scene for evidence gathering.
- Notify a shift supervisor of the incident as soon as practical.
- Do not allow any inmates involved to shower, wash, drink, eat, use toilet facilities, or change clothing until examined.
- Document the incident on an incident report and forward it to a shift supervisor in accordance with facility policy "Reporting of Incidents."

Supervisory Action. In addition to the requirements described above, the supervisor shall:

- Contact the facility duty officer and the local law enforcement authority as soon as practical.
- Alert health services staff as soon as practical. Escort the victim to the health services unit for a private medical and mental health assessment as soon as possible. Health services staff will initiate protocols related to a forensic medical exam.
- Take appropriate steps to ensure that the victim is not left alone.
- Explain to the victim that there is help available to cope with the situation, including outside advocacy support services.
- Offer or arrange for the victim to speak with the facility's religious service representative.
- Complete all necessary reports in accordance with facility policies.

All Employees. Each employee shall:

- Avoid labeling the victim or predator by using slang or inappropriate words.
- Treat a sexual assault incident as a serious and confidential matter.
- Recognize that sexual assault survivors may engage in sexual acts, which may present an appearance of being consensual, out of a desire for protection from violent assaults and to minimize risk of HIV infection.
- Treat known survivors and targets of sexual assault fairly and without discrimination or unfair judgment.
- Become familiar with your area of responsibility and identify vulnerable sites for potential sexual activity.

10. **Evidence Protocol/Securing the Area.** The area of any attempted or actual sexual assault shall be treated as a possible crime scene in accordance with facility policy. Once the inmate is removed from the area, care shall be taken not to disturb the suspected crime scene. Items shall not be cleaned or removed. Photos/video shall be taken of the suspected crime scene and any suspected physical evidence. Sketches and notes should be made of the cell, including the location of items, especially those that have been removed as evidence. Only authorized personnel shall be allowed to enter the area. The collection of physical evidence shall be conducted by the local law enforcement authority or, in instances when authorized by the law enforcement authority, the facility shall collect, secure, and store physical evidence. If required, facility personnel shall collect evidence as follows:

- Latex or rubber gloves shall be used.

- Each specific item of physical evidence shall be placed in a separate paper bag, envelope, or container to avoid disturbing or compromising the integrity of the physical evidence.

- The storage container shall be tagged.

- Physical evidence items, when removed from the scene, shall be placed directly in the physical evidence storage area or turned over to the appropriate law enforcement agency.

- Once the local law enforcement authority has cleared the scene, the facility Administrator or designee may issue the orders for the cell/area to be cleaned and inventoried.

11. **Investigation of Sexual Assaults.** All information related to sexual abuse or assault shall be reported and investigated. The local law enforcement authority shall serve as the investigating authority in all incidents of sexual assault within the facility. The facility's PREA Coordinator and Chief of Security shall assist law enforcement as appropriate and shall conduct an internal investigation into the incident in accordance with facility policy.

In the event that local law enforcement declines to investigate a sexual assault allegation, the Chief of Security may forward the case to the appropriate trained staff for investigation. At the completion of the investigation, the Chief of Security shall forward a copy of the outcomes/findings to the facility Administrator. However, during the investigation, if evidence or information is discovered that corroborates the inmate's allegation of sexual assault, staff shall suspend the investigation at the point of discovery and contact the local law enforcement agency for direction about followup.

12. **Classification.** Victims/alleged victims of sexual assault and predators/alleged predators shall be identified and tracked. Inmates involved in sexual assaults shall be kept separate from each other by means of a separation profile/record notation. Inmates who are identified as sexual predators or potential sexual predators, as determined by the Chief of Security, shall be appropriately housed at the facility (or may be transferred to another facility) for the purposes of separation from potential victims.

13. **Victim Support.** Victims of sexual assault shall be referred to qualified mental health professionals for treatment and followup, as necessary. Health services staff shall make appropriate referrals to a community advocacy group in order to provide additional counseling and support for victims/survivors of sexual assault.

14. **Sexual Assault Response Team (SART).** A SART is composed of four or more individuals and includes one coordinator (management official responsible for oversight), one medical staff person, one security staff person, one mental health professional, and one person designated as the facility Victim Services Coordinator. Each member will have a primary role in responding to reported incidents of sexual abuse and will ensure that policy and procedures are carried out that relate to inmate safety and support for the victim's needs. The SART will serve as an advisory group with the PREA Coordinator to address any issues related to inmate sexual safety and will offer recommendations to enhance the policy and procedures related to this subject.

15. **Predator Management.** Inmates identified as sexual predators shall be managed in accordance with facility policy.

16. **Reporting.** Documentation and reporting of sexual assaults or related behavior shall be as follows:

Internal Reporting. All sexual assaults shall be documented in an incident report in accordance with facility policy and included in the monthly PBMS report. The PBMS report shall list the following categories of sexual assault:

- Alleged sexual assaults.
- Abusive sexual contacts.
- Nonconsensual sexual acts.
- Staff sexual harassment of an inmate.
- Staff sexual misconduct toward an inmate.

Security Tracking. The Chief of Security shall track all allegations of sexual misconduct by staff and inmates, including investigation results and any actions taken by the facility staff, local law enforcement, and/or the courts.

17. **Exceptions.** Any exceptions to the procedures in this policy require prior written approval from the facility Administrator.

Summary

The APEX Change Management Model provides a systemic approach to change, sustaining change, and performance improvement. Using this model as a template enables agencies to custom design strategies and activities that will help them create a roadmap for change and sustain their change efforts. As organizations move along the APEX journey, this model can provide a process for making the trip smoother and helping them arrive at their chosen destination effectively and successfully.

The case material offered here is an example of how to achieve culture change and how to comply with new legislation through the use of the APEX Initiative principles and practices. It shows how an agency can employ change management principles, effective communications planning, and the elements of implementing and sustaining change through a story of one agency's adoption and deployment of the Prison Rape Elimination Act.

Chapter 8: Changing Culture during Challenging Times

Budget cuts, overcrowded prisons, high incarceration rates, job loss fears—these are challenging issues for any correctional system. In the past decade, many state correctional systems have transitioned from a tough-on-crime incarceration mode to one focused on offender reentry. Whether this transition is a reflection of the challenging economic times or the research that indicates that a reentry initiative can reduce recidivism and enhance public safety, the common theme is the same. Correctional agency leaders must be culture change agents for any major change initiative to succeed. This chapter addresses many of the strategies that states have implemented to shift their criminal justice and correctional culture from a primary focus on offender confinement to one of offender community reentry.

Creating a Successful Transformation

To achieve a successful correctional agency transformation, agency leadership must learn about the current state of affairs, recognize that culture change is a deliberate process that involves all stakeholders in the criminal justice system, and steadfastly commit to culture change efforts in support of the agency mission. The following stages illustrate an example of a culture change process involving offender reentry in a state correctional system.

Stage 1: Plan and Assess

The state budget has a significant deficit, and with the department of corrections comprising 7 percent of the budget and encompassing the largest workforce of any state agency, the trend is an increase in costs for managing the state agency. The Governor and legislature must make some drastic cost reductions, and the department of corrections is not exempt. The correctional director recognizes that cost containment and/or reduction is inevitable, and decides to engage the APEX Public Safety Model and its strategies for assessing and planning the organizational culture change that will positively affect the agency's performance.

Stage 2: Define the Goal

The director's main goal is to meet the agency's mission to enhance safety for the public, staff, and offenders. A review of the literature illustrates that meeting this goal has been successful in other state systems with the transition to a reentry initiative. The outcomes of a systems approach to reentry indicate the possibility of a reduction in the incarcerated population, closing of facilities, reductions in operating costs, reduction of incidents in correctional facilities, and, most importantly, a reduction in offender recidivism. In effect, the criminal justice system becomes more collaborative, effective, efficient, and transparent with a vibrant reentry initiative.

Stage 3: Organize for Results

The director decides to commit to a reentry initiative; however, making a decision and implementing it are vastly different efforts. The director commits to being the culture Change Leader and establishes a culture Change Team to develop and implement the new agency strategy.

Build the Right Team

The director's strategy team is a multidisciplinary group of agency leaders who are committed to the overriding goal of public safety and recidivism reduction. The team's objectives include cost containment, population reduction, efficient staff and resource allocation, and a critical review of the criminal justice system, decision points, and drivers that affect the agency's confined population. The team submits weekly reports to the director, highlighting activities that may need the director's direct involvement, such as communicating with government officials, community organizations, labor unions, and other critical support systems. The team establishes the performance measures that will indicate the progress of the culture change efforts.

Engage Stakeholders

The team uses the APEX Change Management Communications Plan format found in *APEX: Building the Model and Beginning the Journey* (another book in the APEX Guidebook series) to identify and analyze the stakeholders who have influence with the reentry initiative. Engaging key stakeholders is critical to successful culture change and the initiative's overall success. Developing a communications plan to better guide stakeholder engagement is essential for any major change initiative. The key stakeholders identified in the communications plan include the agency staff; labor unions; legislators; other state agency officials in the areas of probation/parole, mental health and substance abuse, housing, employment, education, and judicial; the media; community advocacy groups; and the faith-based community. Each stakeholder group has corresponding engagement protocols with defined objectives. The team also learns that the use of advisory committees and community-based reentry councils has been very successful across states in sustaining stakeholder engagement, support, partnerships, and investment in the initiative's success.

Stage 4: Build the Detailed Implementation Plan

The team working on the transformation effort is diligent in planning how to implement the strategy to shift the agency culture to one that embraces reentry. It is critical to plan for the expected results and the possible unwanted results of implementing the strategy. Building good relationships with stakeholders and ensuring that they remain informed and engaged in the efforts may lessen the negative impact of an unexpected event, such as an offender committing a heinous crime after release. Agency leadership must be deliberate and consistent in communicating ongoing implementation efforts and the performance outcomes to reinforce the culture change initiative.

Stage 5: Implement the Change Management Plan

The Change Team uses the implementation timeline to monitor and track its progress with respect to the action steps. A scoreboard is developed and displayed to update regularly. Information on the progress of the reentry program is shared with stakeholders in accordance with the communications plan. Agency leadership works with the Change Leader and Executive Team to address any challenges, resistance, and discontent toward the new policies and practices, and is willing to revise plans when necessary.

Stage 6: Sustain the Change

Sustaining any transformation initiative, especially one as broad-based as reentry, requires that leaders/change agents maintain ongoing communication with stakeholders and reinforce the benefits and results of the efforts to them. When stakeholders are involved in the initiative, see the performance results, believe in the benefits, and personally invest in its success, the agency will have a strong foundation to overcome implementation barriers and sustain the transformation over time and during changes in leadership.

Models for Reentry Initiatives

Many states have embarked on culture and change management initiatives related to offender reentry. In many instances, states were able to gain federal, private, and/or public funding to support their efforts. The following sections offer information and strategies on how various states were able to transform their criminal justice and correctional systems to an offender reentry focus with significant success and benefits.

The National Institute of Corrections (NIC) maintains an extensive collection of publications related to reentry and management of organizational culture change. These publications can be found in NIC's Information Center at *http://nicic.gov/.* The Center sponsors programs focused on reentry, including the Transition from Prison to Community (TPC) Initiative and the Transition from Jail to Community Initiative.

Michigan Prisoner Reentry Initiative

Michigan began its reentry program by reallocating money to avoid asking for extra funds. Then the state received NIC technical assistance funding through the TPC Initiative, JEHT Foundation, and National Governors Association to enlarge the program. The early years looked very successful, with a 23-percent improvement in recidivism. Then the state began working to reduce inmate length of stay: Michigan's inmates served an average of 16 months longer per offense than those in neighboring states. Because Michigan used indeterminate sentencing, there was often a large gap between the minimum sentence (when a prisoner became eligible for parole) and the maximum sentence. The next efforts focused on earlier parole for offenders to reduce prison crowding, and on appeasing the parole boards with more effective community reintegration plans to ensure successful parole petitions. According to the Sentencing Project's report on the downscaling of four prisons in the United States, Michigan realized a 12-percent reduction in the prison population (from 51,577 to 45,478) from 2006 to 2009. Through Michigan's initiative, the parole board began to review the cases of all offenders whose sentences involved only drug or other nonviolent crimes. Once the parole board was assured that there would be adequate support in the community, it agreed to more early parole releases. Because most parolees were able to stay out of prison, this trend continued (Alexander 2009, Greene and Mauer 2010, Mandeville 2004, Mogelson 2010).

Michigan has shown great success with its efforts. A report illustrating the breadth of the initiative stakeholders and results is available at *http://www.michigan.gov/documents/corrections/MPRI_2010_Progress_Report_343664_7.pdf.*

Kentucky Department of Corrections Reentry

The Kentucky Department of Corrections (DOC) introduced its reentry philosophy, the benefits of changing to a reentry model, and the DOC's approach to supporting this philosophy in November 2009. Collaboration and support for the reentry initiative continue to expand and improve. The DOC added staff—facility reentry coordinators along with reentry probation and parole officers—who were dedicated to the reentry program. In addition, the DOC has trained more than 750 staff to incorporate the Level of Services Case Management Inventory (LS–CMI) into case planning, a vital component to managing an offender's risk and assigning him/her to risk-reduction programs and services.

A key element of the agency's reentry approach involves inviting the public to help the agency meet its mission to ensure public safety and reduce recidivism. To educate the public and staff, and to encourage support from stakeholders, the DOC introduced "The Tool Kit" in September 2011 as part of its communications plan. This monthly newsletter informs readers about ongoing collaborative efforts related to reentry, including the names and contact information of staff assigned as reentry coordinators and community supervisors, programs and services available to offenders, success stories of reentry efforts, and updates on the Kentucky Alliance for ReEntry Committee activities.

To access "The Tool Kit" and learn how it is used to reinforce reentry efforts across the state through stakeholder engagement, visit *http://corrections.ky.gov/reentry/Pages/default.aspx*.

Connecticut Department of Correction Reentry Strategy Report

To enhance public safety, in 2003 the leadership of the Connecticut Department of Correction transitioned the agency from a back-to-basics confinement model to one where the mission focus shifted to offender reentry. Connecticut has a unified system in which the state detention facilities, prisons, and community corrections (postincarceration) are all administered under the state Department of Correction. The results of this business model change included a 9-percent reduction in the confined population from 2003 to 2011. Prior to the reentry initiative, the state-projected annual offender population increased along with related budgetary expenses. Since the reentry initiative began, the state has realized a significant savings of over $800 million in cost avoidance. Most importantly, since the reentry strategy was implemented, which led to a reduction in the confined population and an increase in the supervision of offenders in the community, the recidivism rate and the overall state crime rate have declined.

The State of Connecticut Reentry Strategy outlines the state's approach; it was prepared in response to a legislative request and it describes the ongoing collaborative efforts of the state criminal justice agencies and their stakeholders. This document includes guiding principles, reentry goals, stakeholder engagement efforts, programs, and services, as well as an integrated risk reduction case management model. This document is available at *http://www.ct.gov/opm/lib/opm/cjppd/cjcjpac/cjpac_2010_reentry_strategy_(2).pdf*.

The State of Connecticut Risk Assessment Strategy complements the Reentry Strategy. It focuses on collaboration among criminal justice agencies for enhancing public safety with an integrated system of risk assessment and risk management. This document is available at *http://www.ct.gov/doc/lib/doc/risk_assess_strategy_report_2010.pdf*.

The Sentencing Project

The Sentencing Project promotes transformation in sentencing law and practice to reduce the criminal justice system's reliance on incarceration. This organization has several publications that relate to reentry strategies, including *Downscaling Prisons: Lessons from Four States* (Greene and Mauer 2010) and *On the Chopping Block: State Prison Closings* (Porter 2011). These publications and others are available at *www.sentencingproject.org*.

Summary

In these challenging times, as budgets shrink, it remains critical to ensure stakeholder safety. Because of the need to maintain both security and cost efficiency, it has become increasingly important to reduce inmate populations through improving reentry programs, reducing costs, and focusing the correctional organization's culture on higher performance. Change can happen in a correctional organization as the culture becomes more responsive to financial and performance needs. This chapter highlights a model of successful organization change for reentry—the APEX Change Management Process. This chapter also discusses several other models for reentry initiatives that are worthy of study when planning a change initiative.

References

Alexander, E. 2009. *Michigan Breaks the Political Logjam: A New Model for Reducing Prison Populations.* New York: ACLU National Prison Project, *www.aclu.org/files/assets/2009-12-18-MichiganReport.pdf,* accessed October 26, 2011.

Greene, J., and M. Mauer. 2010. *Downscaling Prisons: Lessons from Four States.* Washington, DC: The Sentencing Project, *http://www.sentencingproject.org/doc/publications/publications/inc_DownscalingPrisons2010.pdf,* accessed September 26, 2011.

Mandeville, M. 2004. "Revamping the Inmate Reentry Process in Michigan." Corrections.com (January 19), *http://www.corrections.com/articles/1122-revamping-the-inmate-reentry-process-in-michigan,* accessed September 26, 2011.

Mogelson, L. 2010. "Prison Break." *Washington Monthly* (November/December), *http://www.washingtonmonthly.com/features/2010/1011.mogelson.html,* accessed September 20, 2011.

Porter, N.D. 2011. *On the Chopping Block: State Prisons Closing* (September 15). Washington, DC: The Sentencing Project, *http://sentencingproject.org/doc/publications/On_the_chopping_block_-_state_prison_closings_(2).pdf,* accessed September 26, 2011.

Book Summary

Culture, including the beliefs, assumptions, values, norms, and practices in an organization, determines the success of an organization's performance and change efforts. This book helps illuminate the role culture plays in an organization that is striving for higher performance. A strong sense of where an organization's culture falls on the continuums between external versus internal focus, and between structure and control versus flexibility and agility, determines which of four cultural types the organization is most closely aligned with. The Competing Values Framework helps identify these cultural types and direct an organization toward growth.

Knowledge of culture enables an organization to proceed along the path to successful change. The APEX Change Management Model provides a process and map for organizational change based on research and best practices; it engages the human component of the organization to ensure success. Communication is key to any change effort, and a general blueprint for developing a communication strategy is detailed in this book, along with an example for developing a Prison Rape Elimination Act (PREA) change initiative communications plan. An APEX Change Management Process is included; it is written to model an organization that is shifting its culture to align with PREA standards. As budget cuts hinder correctional operations, the movement to reduce the offender population through safer and more effective reentry programs is increasing. An APEX Change Management Model, written with respect to reentry and case studies of change initiatives, is highlighted in this book.

Bibliography

This bibliography is organized by the following topics:

- Culture

- Change Management

Culture

Barriere, M., B. Anson, R. Ording, and E. Rogers. 2002. "Culture Transformation in a Health Care Organization." *Consulting Psychology Journal: Practice and Research* 54(2).

Bass, B., and B. Avolio. 1994. *Improving Organizational Effectiveness through Transformational Leadership.* Thousand Oaks, CA: Sage Publications.

Blake, R., and J. Mouton. 1964. *The Managerial Grid: The Key to Leadership Excellence.* Houston: Gulf Publishing Company.

Boan, D. 2006. "Cognitive Behavior Modification and Organizational Culture." *Consulting Psychology Journal: Practice and Research* (Winter).

Bogue, B. 2010. "How Principles of High Reliability Organizations Relate to Corrections." *Federal Probation* 73:22–27.

Boonstra, J. 2004. "Dynamics of Organization Change and Learning: Reflections and Perspectives." In J. Boonstra (ed.), *Dynamics of Organizational Change and Learning.* Chichester, England: Wiley Books.

Bradley, L., and R. Parker. 2000. *Organisational Culture in the Public Sector.* Queensland, Australia: The Institute of Public Administration, *http://unpan1.un.org/intradoc/groups/public/documents/apcity/unpan006307.pdf,* accessed January 24, 2012.

Burke, W., M. Waclawski, and J. Church. 1993. "The Dynamics of Midstream Consulting." *Consulting Psychology Journal* (Winter).

Cameron, K. 2008. *Positive Leadership: Strategies for Extraordinary Performance.* San Francisco: Berrett-Koehler.

Cameron, K., J. Dutton, and R. Quinn. 2003. *Positive Organizational Scholarship: Foundations of a New Discipline.* San Francisco: Berrett-Kohler.

Cameron, K., and R. Quinn. 1999. "An Introduction to Changing Organizational Culture." In *Diagnosing and Changing Organizational Culture Based on the Competing Values Framework.* San Francisco: Jossey-Bass.

Cameron, K., and R. Quinn. 2006. *Diagnosing and Changing Organizational Culture.* San Francisco: Jossey-Bass.

Carmeli, A., and A. Tishler. 2004. "The Relationship Between Intangible Organizational Elements and Organizational Performance." *Strategic Management Journal* 25(13):1257–78.

Cooke, R.A., and D.M. Rousseau. 1988. "Behavioral Norms and Expectations: A Quantitative Approach to the Assessment of Organizational Culture." *Group and Organization Studies* 13(3).

Davies, H.T.O., S. Nutley, and R. Mannion. 2000. "Organizational Culture and Quality of Health Care." *Quality Health Care* 9.

Dees, J.G., B. Battle-Anderson, and J. Wei-Skillern. 2004. "Scaling Social Impact." *Stanford Social Innovation Review* 1(4).

Denison, D. 1996. "What is the Difference between Organizational Culture and Organizational Climate?" *Academy of Management Review* 21:619–54.

Eccles, M.P., and B.S. Mittman. 2006. "Welcome to Implementation Science." *Implementation Science* 1(1).

Eggers, J., and J. Gray. 2012. "Leadership That is Transforming." In N. Cebula, E. Craig, J. Eggers, M. Fajardo, J. Gray, and T. Lantz (eds.), *Achieving Performance Excellence: The Influence of Leadership on Organizational Performance.* Washington, DC: U.S. Department of Justice, National Institute of Corrections.

Elliott, D., S. Mihalic, and A. Fagan. 2001. *The Importance of Implementation Fidelity.* Boulder, CO: Center for the Study and Prevention of Violence.

Farber, B.A., and E.M. Doolin. 2011. "Positive Regard." *Psychotherapy* 48(1):58–64.

Fixsen, D., S. Naoom, K. Blase, R. Friedman, and F. Wallace. 2005. *Implementation Research: A Synthesis of the Literature.* Tampa, FL: National Implementation Research Network.

Flaherty-Zonis, C. 2007. *Building Culture Strategically: A Team Approach for Corrections.* Washington, DC: U.S. Department of Justice, National Institute of Corrections.

Heckscher, C. 2006. "Organizations, Movements, and Networks." *New York Law School Review* 5(2):313–36.

Holman, P. 2010. *Engaging Emergence.* San Francisco: Berrett-Koehler.

Hooijberg, R., and J. Choi. 2001. "The Impact of Organizational Characteristics on Leadership Effectiveness Models: An Examination of Leadership in a Private and a Public Sector Organization." *Administration & Society* 33(4).

Kegan, R., and L. Lahey. 2009. *Immunity to Change.* Boston: Harvard Business Press.

Koenigs, R.H., S. Hare, A.P. Hare, and M. Cowan. 2004. *SYMLOG Reliability and Validity.* Woodland Hills, CA: SYMLOG Consulting Group.

Kotter, J. 1995. "Leading Change: Why Transformation Efforts Fail." *Harvard Business Review OnPoint* (March-April).

Kotter, J., and H. Rathgeber. 2006. *Our Iceberg Is Melting.* New York: St. Martin's Press.

Kuratko, D.F., R.V. Montagno, and J.S. Hornsby. 1990. "Developing an Intrapreneunerial Assessment Instrument for an Effective Corporate Entrepreneurial Environment." *Strategic Management Journal* 11.

Levesque, D., J. Prochaska, and J. Prochaska. 1999. "Stages of Change and Integrated Service Delivery." *Consulting Psychology Journal: Practice and Research* 51(4).

Lewin, K. 1947. "Frontiers in Group Dynamics II: Channels of Group Life; Social Planning and Action Research." *Human Relations* (November):143–53.

Likert, R. 1961. *New Patterns of Management.* New York: McGraw-Hill Book Company

Lusthaus, C., M.H. Adrien, G. Anderson, F. Carden, and G. Plinio Montalvan. 2002. *Organizational Assessment: A Framework for Improving Performance.* Ottawa, Canada: International Development Research Centre.

Marlett, G.A., and J. Gordon. 1985. *Relapse Prevention.* New York: Guilford Press.

Mihalic, S., K. Irwin, A. Fagan, D. Ballard, and D. Elliott. 2004. *Successful Program Implementation: Lessons From Blueprints.* Washington, DC: U.S. Department of Justice, Office of Justice Programs, Office of Juvenile Justice and Delinquency Prevention.

Miller, W., A. Zweben, C. DiClemente, and R. Rychtarik. 1995. *Motivational Enhancement Therapy Manual.* Rockville, MD: National Institute on Alcohol Abuse and Alcoholism.

Muhlau, P., and R. Wittek. 2003. "A Structural Theory of Punishment Centered Organizational Culture." Paper presented at the annual meeting of the American Sociological Association.

Parker, C.P., B.B. Baltes, S.A. Young, J.W. Huff, R.A. Altermann, H.A. Lacost, and J.E. Roberts. 2003. "Relationships Between Psychological Climate Perceptions and Work Outcomes: A Meta-analytic Review." *Journal of Organizational Behavior* 24.

Pascale, R., M. Millemann, and L. Gioja. 1997. "Changing the Way We Change." *Harvard Business Review OnPoint* (November-December).

Pascale, R., and J. Sternin. 2005. "Your Company's Secret Change Agents." *Harvard Business Review OnPoint* (May).

Peterson, M.F., and S.L. Castro. 2006. "Measurement Metrics at Aggregate Levels of Analysis: Implications for Organization Culture Research and the GLOBE Project." *Science Direct: The Leadership Quarterly* 17.

Prochaska, J., and C. DiClemente. 1984. *The Transtheoretical Approach: Crossing the Traditional Boundaries of Therapy.* Melbourne, FL: Krieger Publishing Company.

Prochaska, J.O., J.C. Norcross, and C.C. DiClemente. 1994. *Changing for Good.* New York: Morrow.

Prochaska, J.O., and J.C. Norcross. 2006. *Systems of Psychotherapy: A Transtheoretical Analysis.* Pacific Grove, CA: Brooks-Cole.

Rehm, R. 1999. *People in Charge: Creating Self Managing Workplaces.* Gloucestershire, England: Hawthorn Press.

Rehm, R., N. Cebula., F. Ryan, and M. Large. 2002. *Futures That Work: Using Search Conferences to Revitalize Companies, Communities and Organizations.* Gabriola Island, British Columbia, Canada: New Society Publishers.

Rentsch, J., and J. Klimoski. 2001. "Why Do Great Minds Think Alike? Antecedents of Team Member Schema Agreement." *Journal of Organizational Behavior* 22(2).

Schein, E. 1999. *The Corporate Culture Survival Guide.* San Francisco: Jossey-Bass.

Schein, E. 2004. *Organizational Culture and Leadership.* San Francisco: Jossey-Bass.

Schein, E.H. 2005. *Organizational Culture and Leadership,* 3d ed. San Francisco: Jossey-Bass.

Simpson, D. 2002. "A Conceptual Framework for Transferring Research to Practice." *Journal of Substance Abuse Treatment* 22(4):171–82.

Smith, T.B., Rodriguez, M.D., and G. Bernal. 2011. "Culture." *Journal of Clinical Psychology* 67(2):166–75.

Ulmer, J., and B. Johnson. 2004. "Sentencing in Context: A Multilevel Analysis." *Criminology* 42(1).

Weick, K., and K. Sutcliffe. 2001. *Managing the Unexpected: Assuring High Performance in an Age of Complexity.* San Francisco: Jossey-Bass.

White, L. 2000. "Changing the Whole System in the Public Sector." *Journal of Organizational Change Management* 13.

Yauch, C., and H. Steudel. 2003. "Complementary Use of Qualitative and Quantitative Cultural Assessment Methods." *Organizational Research Methods* 6(4).

Change Management

Aiman-Smith, L. 2004. *What Do We Know About Developing and Sustaining a Culture of Innovation.* Raleigh, NC: North Carolina State University.

Alexander, E. 2009. *Michigan Breaks the Political Logjam: A New Mode for Reducing Prison Populations.* New York: ACLU National Prison Project, *www.aclu.org/files/assets/2009-12-18-MichiganReport.pdf,* accessed October 26, 2011.

Association of State Correctional Administrators. 2008. *Performance Based Measurements System.* Hagerstown, MD: Association of State Correctional Administrators, *http://nicic.gov/Library/021116,* accessed December 2, 2011.

Axelrod, R. 2010. *Terms of Engagement.* San Francisco: Berrett-Koehler.

Backer, T.E., and R.P. Liberman. 1986. "Dissemination and Adoption of Innovative Psychosocial Interventions." *Journal of Consulting Psychology* 54(February):111–18.

Baker, K.A. 2002. "Innovation." In *The Management Benchmark Study.* Washington, DC: Department of Energy Office of Science, Air University (USAF), *http://www.au.af.mil/au/awc/awcgate/doe/benchmark/ch14.pdf,* accessed May 25, 2010.

Baldrige National Quality Program. 2011. *Criteria for Performance Excellence.* Gaithersburg, MD: National Institute of Standards and Technology.

Bartholomew, N., G. Joe, G. Rowan-Szal, and D. Simpson. 2007. "Counselor Assessments of Training and Adoption Barriers." *Journal of Substance Abuse Treatment* 25(June):252–61.

Beckhard, R., and W. Pritchard. 1992. *Changing the Essence.* San Francisco: Jossey-Bass.

Bozeman, B. 2000. "Technology Transfer and Public Policy: A Review of Research and Theory." *Research Policy* 29:627–55.

Broom, K, P. Flynn, D. Knight, and D. Simpson. 2007. "Program Structure, Staff Perceptions and Client Engagement in Treatment." *Journal of Substance Abuse Treatment* 33(2):149–58.

Cameron, K., and R. Quinn. 2006. *Diagnosing and Changing Organizational Culture.* San Francisco: Jossey-Bass.

Campbell, J. 2004. "What's New? General Patterns of Planned Macro-Institutional Change." Paper presented to the American Sociological Association, San Francisco, August 14.

Carr, A. 1997. "The Learning Organization: New Lessons/Thinking for the Management of Change and Management Development?" *Journal of Management Development* 16(4):224–31.

Castells, M. 2000. "Toward a Sociology of the Network Society." *Contemporary Sociology* 29(5):693–99.

Christensen, C.M., H. Baumann, R. Ruggles, and M.T. Sadtler. 2006. *Disruptive Innovation for Social Change.* Watertown, MA: Harvard Business Review.

Clarke, G.N. 1995. "Improving the Transition from Basic Efficacy Research to Effectiveness Studies: Methodological Issues and Procedures." *Journal of Consulting and Clinical Psychology* 63(5):718–25.

Cognitive Edge. 2006. "The Future, Backwards," *http://www.cognitive-edge.com/files/Future-Backwards.pdf,* accessed December 2, 2011.

Corrigan, P.W., L. Stiener, G.S. McCracken, B. Blaser, and M. Barr. 2001. "Strategies for Disseminating Evidence-Based Practices to Staff Who Treat People with Serious Mental Illness." *Psychiatric Services* 52(December):1598–1606.

Davis, S.M. 1982. "Transforming Organizations: The Key to Strategy is Context." *Organizational Dynamics* (Winter):64–80.

Dechenaux, E., B. Goldfarb, S. Shane, and M. Thursby. 2003. *Appropriability and the Timing of Innovation Evidence from MIT Inventions.* Cambridge, MA: NBER Working Paper Series, British Library Direct.

Drucker, P. 2002. "The Discipline of Innovation." *Harvard Business Review* (August).

Elliott, D., S. Mihalic, and A. Fagan. 2001. *The Importance of Implementation Fidelity.* Boulder, CO: University of Colorado at Boulder, Institute of Behavioral Sciences, Center for the Study and Prevention of Violence.

Farabee, D., M.L. Prendergast, J. Cartier, H. Wexler, K. Knight, and D. Anglin. 1999. "Barriers to Implementing Effective Correctional Drug Treatment Programs." *The Prison Journal* 79(2):150–62.

Fixsen, D., S. Naoom, K. Blase, R. Friedman, and F. Wallace. 2005. *Implementation Research: A Synthesis of the Literature.* Tampa, FL: University of South Florida.

Geffen, M., and J. Kost. 2006. *How Technology Enables Transformation of Human Service Administration.* Washington, DC: Policy & Practice of Public Human Services.

Gladwell, M. 2000. *The Tipping Point: How Little Things Make a Big Difference.* New York: Little, Brown and Company.

Greene, J., and M. Mauer. 2010. *Downscaling Prisons: Lessons from Four States.* Washington, DC: The Sentencing Project, *http://www.sentencingproject.org/doc/publications/publications/inc_DownscalingPrisons2010.pdf,* accessed September 26, 2011.

Greenhalgh, T., R. Glenn, F. MacFarlane, P. Bate, and O. Kyirakidou. 2004. "Diffusion of Innovations in Service Organizations: Systemic Review and Recommendations." *The Millbank Quarterly* 82(4).

Harvard Business Review. 2006. *Leading Through Change.* Boston: Harvard Business School Press.

Heerwagen, J.H. 2002. "Creativity." In *The Management Benchmark Study.* Washington, DC: Department of Energy Office of Science, Air University (USAF), *http://www.au.af.mil/au/awc/awcgate/doe/benchmark/ch15.pdf,* accessed January 24, 2012.

Hesselbein, F., and R. Johnson. 2002. *On Leading Change.* San Francisco: Jossey-Bass.

Hiatt, J.M. 2006. *ADKAR: A Model for Change in Business, Government and Our Community.* Loveland, CO: Prosci.

Holman, P., T. Devane, and S. Cady. 2007. *The Change Handbook.* San Francisco: Berrett-Koehler.

Hultman, K. 1998. *Making Change Irresistible.* Palo Alto, CA: Davies-Black.

Hutton, D. 1994. *The Change Agent's Handbook.* Milwaukee, WI: ASQC Quality Press.

Koppel, T. 1999. *The Deep Dive.* New York: ABC News Nightline (DVD).

Kotter, J. 1996. *Leading Change.* Boston: Harvard Business School Press.

Kotter, J. 2007. "Leading Change: Why Transformation Efforts Fail." *Harvard Business Review* (January):96–103.

Kotter, J.P., and D.S. Cohen. 2002. *The Heart of Change.* Boston: Harvard Business School Press.

Kotter, J., and H. Rathgeber. 2006. *Our Iceberg Is Melting.* New York: St. Martin's Press.

Kubler-Ross, E. 1997. *On Death and Dying.* New York: Scribner.

Kurz, C., and D. Snowden. 2003. "The New Dynamics of Strategy: Sense-making in a Complex and Complicated World," *IBM Systems Journal* 42(3).

Levasseur, R.E. 2009. "People Skills: Implementing Strategic Goals—A Change Management Perspective." *Interfaces* 39(4):370–72.

Levasseur, R.E. 2010. "People Skills: Ensuring Project Success—A Change Management Perspective." *Interfaces* 40(2).

Lloyd, S.R., and I.M. Halasz. 1999. *Building Teams: Skills for the Effective Team Leader.* Washington, DC: American Media, Inc. and the American Correctional Association.

Maginn, M. 2007. *Managing in Times of Change.* New York: McGraw-Hill.

Mandeville, M. 2004. "Revamping the Inmate Reentry Process in Michigan." Corrections.com (January 19), *http://www.corrections.com/articles/1122-revamping-the-inmate-reentry-process-in-michigan,* accessed September 26, 2011.

Mihalic, S., and K. Irwin. 2003. "Blueprints for Violence Prevention: From Research to Real World Setting—Factors Influencing the Successful Replication of Model Programs." *Youth Violence and Juvenile Justice* 1(4): 307–29.

Mihalic, S., K. Irwin, A. Fagan, D. Ballard, and D. Elliott. 2004. *Successful Program Implementation: Lessons From Blueprints.* Washington, DC: U.S. Department of Justice, Office of Justice Programs, Office of Juvenile Justice and Delinquency Prevention.

Mogelson, L. 2010. "Prison Break." *Washington Monthly* (November/December), *http://www.washingtonmonthly. com/features/2010/1011.mogelson.html,* accessed September 20, 2011.

Nutley, S., I. Walter, and H. Davies. 2002. *From Knowing to Doing: A Framework for Understanding the Evidence-into-Practice Agenda.* Edinburgh, Scotland: University of St. Andrews, Research Unit for Research Utilisation.

Ortega-Courtney, K., G. Joe, G. Rowan-Szal, and D. Simpson. 2007. "Using Organizational Assessment as a Tool for Program Change." *Journal of Substance Abuse Treatment* 33(2):131–37.

Porter, N.D. 2011. *On the Chopping Block: State Prisons Closing.* Washington, DC: The Sentencing Project, *http://sentencingproject.org/doc/publications/On_the_chopping_block_-_state_prison_closings_(2).pdf,* accessed September 26, 2011.

Rehm, R. 1999. *People in Charge: Creating Self Managing Workplaces.* Gloucestershire, England: Hawthorn Press.

Rehm, R., N. Cebula, F. Ryan, and M. Large. 2002. *Futures that Work: Using Search Conferences to Revitalize Companies, Communities and Organizations.* Gabriola Island, British Columbia, Canada: New Society Publishers.

Robertson, P., and S. Seneviratne. 1995. "Outcomes of Planned Organizational Change in the Public Sector: A Meta-Analytic Comparison to the Private Sector." *Public Administration Review* 55(6):547–58.

Robison, J. 2011. "Overcoming the Fear of Change." *Gallup Management Journal* (January), *http://gmj.gallup.com/content/145484/overcoming-fear-change.aspx,* accessed January 24, 2012.

Rogers, E. 2003. *Diffusion of Innovations.* New York: Free Press.

Rosenheck, R.A. 2001. "Organizational Process: A Missing Link between Research and Practice." *Psychiatric Services* 52(12).

Rowan-Szal, G., J. Greener, G. Joe, and D. Simpson. 2007. "Assessing Program Needs and Planning Change." *Journal of Substance Abuse Treatment* 33(2):121–29.

Saldana, L., J. Chapman, S. Henggeler, and M. Rowland. 2007. "The Organizational Readiness for Change Scale in Adolescent Programs: Criterion Validity." *Journal of Substance Abuse Treatment* 33(2):159–69.

Saveri, A., H. Reingold, and K. Vian. 2005. *Technologies of Cooperation.* Palo Alto, CA: Institute for the Future.

Senge, P. 1999. *The Dance of Change.* New York: Doubleday.

Simpson, D. 2002. "A Conceptual Framework for Transferring Research to Practice." *Journal of Substance Abuse Treatment* 22(4):171–82.

Simpson, D., and P. Flynn. 2007. "Moving Innovations into Treatment: A Stage-Based Approach to Program Change." *Journal of Substance Abuse Treatment* 33(2):111–20.

Simpson, D., G. Joe, and G. Rowan-Szal. 2007. "Linking the Elements of Change: Program and Client Responses to Innovation." *Journal of Substance Abuse Treatment* 33(2):201–09.

Skinner, B.F. 1972. *Beyond Freedom and Dignity.* New York: Alfred A. Knopf.

Sutton, R. 2003. "Sparking Nonprofit Innovation." *Stanford Social Innovation Review* 1(1).

Tsai, H., and M. Yamin. 2006. *Organizational Influences on Innovation Transfer in Multinational Corporations.* Manchester, England: University of Manchester, Manchester Business School.

Tsui, E. 2002. *Technologies for Personal and Peer to Peer (P2P) Knowledge Management.* North Sydney, Australia: Computer Sciences Corporation Leading Edge Forum.

Wejnert, B. 2002. "Integrating Models of Diffusion of Innovations: A Conceptual Framework." *Annual Review of Sociology* 28.

Zald, M. 2004. "Making Change: Why Does the Social Sector Need Social Movements?" *Stanford Social Innovation Review* 2(1).

Afterword

The APEX Guidebook Series

APEX: Building the Model and Beginning the Journey

Culture and Change Management: Using APEX To Facilitate Organizational Change

Achieving Performance Excellence: The Influence of Leadership on Organizational Performance

Understanding Corrections through the APEX Lens

Applying the APEX Tools for Organizational Assessment

APEX Resources Directory Volume 1

APEX Resources Directory Volume 2

About the Authors

Nancy Cebula is the owner of and principal consultant with People in Charge. She has been working as a change agent since the 1970s, from early work as a juvenile probation officer to large systems change work as an organization development consultant. She works with clients in the public and private sectors in the United States and internationally. Nancy is a coauthor and contributor to several books, including *Futures that Work: Using the Search Conference to Revitalize Companies, Communities, and Organizations.* The focus of her work is to help groups of people work together to build strong and vibrant organizations through participative planning, work design, change management, and organizational learning.

Elizabeth Craig is the Manager of the NIC Information Center. Her previous experience includes the design and facilitation of training programs with correctional agencies throughout the United States and consultation on implementation planning and program evaluation. Through her work with innovative national demonstration projects, Elizabeth facilitated ongoing collaboration between public, private, and nonprofit entities in program design and implementation, developing a communication and referral network of national leaders in criminal justice, public health, academia, and clinical health care.

Christopher A. Innes, Ph.D., is the Chief of Research and Information Services at NIC. Since 1985, he has served in a variety of research and policy positions within the Department of Justice. Dr. Innes's past research has focused primarily on jails and prisons, violence and inmate misconduct in correctional institutions, and evaluations of inmate programs. His more recent work at NIC has focused on developing and implementing innovative approaches to managing correctional systems and populations, criminal justice policy, the use of research to inform correctional decisionmaking and practices, and the application of information technology to inform correctional practice.

Theresa Lantz has more than 35 years of experience in the correctional field. Beginning her career as a correctional officer, she served in many public service roles, including counselor, training director, NIC program specialist, warden, and deputy commissioner, culminating with her appointment as the Commissioner of the Connecticut Department of Correction for more than 6 years. Since retiring from full-time public service in 2009, Theresa has been a criminal justice consultant on training, expert witness issues, facility operation and audits, and project development.

Tanya Rhone is the founder and principal of Two Roads Consulting, offering guidance in organizational excellence, leadership, marketing, and strategic planning since 1999. She has more than 20 years of experience honing her leadership skills at Starbucks Coffee Company, The Clorox Company, Paragon Trade Brands, and Weyerhaeuser. With a passion for leadership development, Tanya brings a rich background of facilitation, coaching, training, and organizational design experience to her custom-designed programs and client engagements. She has a deep appreciation for the issues facing today's leaders and the need to ensure proper business focus and results from the investment in learning and development.

Tom Ward has more than 35 years of experience in organizational development, change management, and program and operations management in public, private, and nonprofit organizations. His recent work has involved consulting work with senior management teams and policy as well as operational staff in the U.S. Marine Corps, the U.S. Navy, and the National Archives. Areas of consulting and research emphasis include large-scale organizational change, development of high-performance executive leadership teams, project and change management, workforce engagement, organizational work culture, and design and delivery of leadership development programs.

U.S. Department of Justice

National Institute of Corrections

Washington, DC 20534

Official Business
Penalty for Private Use $300

Address Service Requested

Western Illinois University
School of Law Enforcement and Justice Administration
LEJA 520 Course Syllabus

Course Information
Course Title: Restorative Justice
Course Number: LEJA 520

Faculty Information
Name: Barry S. McCrary, Ed.D.
Phone Number: 309-298-1220
E-mail: bs-mccrary@wiu.edu

Course Description:

This course reviews the evolution and development of what has come to be known as Restorative Justice. The learning experience will address a variety of topics including restorative justice principles, community engagement, victim issues, and restorative practices and change. This workbook is a collection of various articles for class discussion and research.

Upon completion of this course, our graduates will be able to:

1. Demonstrate an understanding of restorative justice concepts, principles, and values.
2. Recognize the traumatic impact of crime on victims, communities, and offenders, and ways to be responsive to the needs and interest of crime victims.
3. Explain the configuration, methods, and potential uses of various restorative practices and evaluate the degree to which they are more or less restorative.
4. Identify several practical strategies for developing active partnerships within the community.
5. Manage personal, interpersonal, and organizational change and prepare strategies for addressing the response to change efforts.
6. Develop the first steps of a plan of action.

Module *Six: Develop the first steps of a plan of action.*	
	Details
Objectives	**1.1** Assess your local jurisdiction's progress or readiness to move toward a restorative framework or model in relationship to the practices. **1.2** Identify a priority goal or objective for local jurisdiction or program and determine first action to take toward achieving that goal or objectives. **1.3** Select appropriate participants for the action planning process and describe potential benefits and losses to each of the participants. **1.4** Determine the impact of stakeholders on proposed changes in your jurisdiction, and the extent to which these stakeholders will aid or impede the process. **1.5** Implement your first step actions within an agreed on time frame, and continue the action plan process with key stakeholders in your jurisdiction.

Successful Implementation of Restorative Justice Practices

By Joseph B. Urban / Dec 20, 2016

The passage of legislation mandating consideration of Restorative Justice in schools marks a movement away from "zero tolerance" by requiring schools to consider a number of mitigating factors or alternatives before suspending or expelling students. We describe the bills themselves and their requirements in a previous e-alert, which may be accessed here. We will also host a webinar with Restorative Justice expert Nancy Schertzing on January 4, 2017 from 12 PM to 12:45 PM. Click here to register for this complimentary webinar.

Put simply, Restorative Justice is a philosophy and disciplinary practice that defines accountability as healing the harm rather than taking the punishment. It brings together those who cause harm with those they've hurt in facilitated interventions designed to acknowledge the harm and identify appropriate actions to make things right as much as possible. This makes Restorative Justice a developmental tool for addressing conflict and misconduct by fostering empathy, personal responsibility and community-building. Schools that have integrated Restorative Justice philosophy and practices into their cultures have experienced precipitous drops in discipline referrals and significant improvements in safety.

Any time a specific approach to discipline is legislated, the first step toward compliance is a change in the prevailing thoughts on implementation of compliance measures. School communities should familiarize themselves with the considerations this legislation mandates before disciplining a student, whether through exclusion or Restorative Practices. The time and effort schools invest in integrating Restorative Justice principles will yield safer, more unified learning communities and inoculate them from challenges invited by the bills, which are discussed below.

One such challenge is a collateral attack on the discipline itself. While previously the only check on disciplinary action was that the fundamentals of due process be applied, the Restorative Justice bills require that, in addition to simply providing due process, the school (and, therefore, the administrator) must consider mitigating factors, including whether to apply Restorative Justice principles. This fundamental shift from zero tolerance might seem daunting, but it can be implemented with fidelity if several best practices are undertaken.

First, it is important to understand what is required. The bills make it a "rebuttable presumption" that suspension of more than 10 days or expulsion is not justified unless the disciplinary officer or tribunal considered the following mitigating factors related to the pupil: age, disciplinary history, disability, seriousness of the behavior, whether the behavior threatened the safety of students or staff, whether Restorative Practices will be used and whether a lesser intervention would be appropriate. The term "rebuttable presumption" means a "presumption which may be rebutted by evidence." Blacks Law Dictionary. Thus, before invoking long-term suspension or expulsion, a school district must demonstrate that it considered the mitigating factors or it risks creating a situation where its decision could be questioned or deemed unjustified. While the bills speak in terms of granting discretion to the local board or administrator, some might say they actually circumscribe the discretion already possessed.

If they wish to avoid challenges to their discipline, boards and administrators must create an environment where the Restorative Justice philosophy embodied in the bills can be fostered. To implement a Restorative Justice program, experts and the MDE suggest that school leadership:

> Adopt a restorative philosophy toward educating and disciplining students;
> Train administrators, counselors and safety officers in the Restorative Justice philosophy and practices for resolving conflict and addressing misconduct;
> Establish a method of data collection to demonstrate fidelity and measure changes in student conduct;
> Obtain staff buy in on the restorative philosophy and systemic approach;
> Identify a core team to help integrate the process and ensure fidelity in implementation;
> Train staff on Restorative Justice philosophy and general practices; and
> Gather and review quantitative and qualitative data to constantly assess and improve.

To maintain a program demonstrably faithful to Restorative Justice principles, a robust professional development program should be considered. The program should include training from experts in the Restorative Justice process, development of procedures for consideration in disciplinary infractions (such as referral sheets that include documented consideration of the mitigating factors set forth in the bills), re-drafting of student handbooks to align with the bills, and implementing staff-wide in-services to introduce Restorative Justice and explain the new legal requirements.

These bills take effect August 1, 2017, allowing plenty of time to plan for the smooth implementation of the mandates and the Restorative Justice principles they envision. Clark Hill and our partners stand ready to help in this process. Future e-alerts will detail specific best practices drawn from the MDE. Again, on January 4, 2017, we will offer a webinar outlining this legislation and the basics of Restorative Justice. We hope you will join us to learn more.

Western Illinois University
School of Law Enforcement and Justice Administration
LEJA 520 Course Syllabus

Course Information
Course Title: Restorative Justice
Course Number: LEJA 520

Faculty Information
Name: Barry S. McCrary, Ed.D.
Phone Number: 309-298-1220
E-mail: bs-mccrary@wiu.edu

Course Description:

This course reviews the evolution and development of what has come to be known as Restorative Justice. The learning experience will address a variety of topics including restorative justice principles, community engagement, victim issues, and restorative practices and change. This workbook is a collection of various articles for class discussion and research.

Course Learning Outcomes

Upon completion of this course, our graduates will be able to:

1. Demonstrate an understanding of restorative justice concepts, principles, and values.
2. Recognize the traumatic impact of crime on victims, communities, and offenders, and ways to be responsive to the needs and interest of crime victims.
3. Explain the configuration, methods, and potential uses of various restorative practices and evaluate the degree to which they are more or less restorative.
4. Identify several practical strategies for developing active partnerships within the community.
5. Manage personal, interpersonal, and organizational change and prepare strategies for addressing the response to change efforts.
6. Develop the first steps of a plan of action.

Module *Seven: Restorative justice research and practical application*

	Details
Objectives	**1.1** Discover the meaning and defining features of community. **1.2** Described the importance of community involvement in restorative efforts. **1.3** Describe the impact of culture diversity on community building. **1.4** Determine ways in which partnerships between the criminal justice system and the community can be built.

Western Illinois University
School of Law Enforcement and Justice Administration
LEJA 520 Course Syllabus

Course Information
Course Title: Restorative Justice
Course Number: LEJA 520

Faculty Information
Name: Barry S. McCrary, Ed.D.
Phone Number: 309-298-1220
E-mail: bs-mccrary@wiu.edu

Course Description:

This course reviews the evolution and development of what has come to be known as Restorative Justice. The learning experience will address a variety of topics including restorative justice principles, community engagement, victim issues, and restorative practices and change. This workbook is a collection of various articles for class discussion and research.

Upon completion of this course, our graduates will be able to:

1. Demonstrate an understanding of restorative justice concepts, principles, and values.
2. Recognize the traumatic impact of crime on victims, communities, and offenders, and ways to be responsive to the needs and interest of crime victims.
3. Explain the configuration, methods, and potential uses of various restorative practices and evaluate the degree to which they are more or less restorative.
4. Identify several practical strategies for developing active partnerships within the community.
5. Manage personal, interpersonal, and organizational change and prepare strategies for addressing the response to change efforts.
6. Develop the first steps of a plan of action.

Module *Eight: International restorative justice initiatives*

Details	Due
1.1 Identify the elements present in an effective conflict resolution process. **1.2** Describe the principles and values of restorative justice. **1.3** Name the three primary stakeholders in the restorative justice process. **1.4** Describe the role of accountability in restorative justice process.	